MW016 4602

A Sociological Worldview

Essentials of Sociology

First Edition

Evelyn Reynolds

Parkland College

 cognella®

SAN DIEGO

Bassim Hamadeh, CEO and Publisher
Angela Schultz, Senior Field Acquisitions Editor
Craig Lincoln, Project Editor
Abbey Hastings, Senior Production Editor
Jessica Delia, Graphic Design Associate
Laura Duncan, Licensing Coordinator
Natalie Piccotti, Director of Marketing
Kassie Graves, Vice President of Editorial
Alia Bales, Director of Editorial and Production

Copyright © 2025 by Cognella, Inc. All rights reserved. No part of this publication may be reprinted, reproduced, transmitted, or utilized in any form or by any electronic, mechanical, or other means, now known or hereafter invented, including photocopying, microfilming, and recording, or in any information retrieval system without the written permission of Cognella, Inc. For inquiries regarding permissions, translations, foreign rights, audio rights, and any other forms of reproduction, please contact the Cognella Licensing Department at rights@cognella.com.

Trademark Notice: Product or corporate names may be trademarks or registered trademarks and are used only for identification and explanation without intent to infringe.

Cover image: Copyright © 2018 iStockphoto LP/gremlin.

Printed in the United States of America.

cognella® | ACADEMIC PUBLISHING
3970 Sorrento Valley Blvd., Ste. 500, San Diego, CA 92121

Brief Contents

Table of Contents

Health Care in Cuba *104*
Applying Sociology: Which Place Would I Rather Grow Old? *104*
The Social Implications of Age in Population Dynamics 105
The Social Construction of Ageism 106
Summary: Connecting the Pieces 107
Review and Critical Thinking 108

Chapter 10. **Geopolitical Economy** **109**
The *Unmighty* Dollar? 109
Chapter Objectives 110
Key Terms 111
Major Political Systems of the World 111
Authoritarian Political Systems *111*
Democratic Political Systems *112*
Political Parties and Elections 113
Major Economic Systems of the World 115
Mixed Economies *115*
Capitalist Systems *116*
Socialist Systems *117*
The Geopolitics of Development 117
The Emergence of Multipolarity 119
Applying Sociology: Examine a Country Through a Geopolitical Economy Lens *119*
Summary: Connecting the Pieces 120
Review and Critical Thinking 120

Chapter 11. **Education and Religion** **121**
How Separate are Church and State? 121
Chapter Objectives 122
Key Terms 123
Education as a Social Institution 123
Education, Democracy, and Capitalism 123
Major Religions of the World 125
Christianity *125*
Islam *125*
Hinduism *126*
The Politics of Religion 126
Applying Sociology: Connecting Views on Education and Religion to Theory *127*
Theoretical Perspectives on Education and Religion 128
Summary: Connecting the Pieces 128
Review and Critical Thinking 129

CHAPTER 1

A Sociological Worldview

Image 1.1

What does it mean to be a *citizen of the world*? The actor, musician, and activist Paul Robeson was deemed "a citizen of the world" not only because he was world-renown, but also because of his investment and concern for his local and national communities.

A sociological worldview involves not only an analysis of our surrounding social arrangements, behaviors, and ideas, but an understanding of how we as individuals, and as a nation, are connected to other individuals and nations around the world.

The United States is not an isolated, autonomous stretch of land. North America (separate from South/Latin America) is actually one of the smallest continents, making up only about 5% of the world population. Major social occurrences, such as colonialism, slavery, industrial revolutions, and science and technology advancement, have made the world's continents and countries much more interactive and interdependent than ever before. Contemporary global crises like war and health pandemics reveal the fact that what happens in one part of the world impacts its other parts.

The sociological perspective can make us more aware and informed of the larger world around us and our particular place in it. To paraphrase the words of sociologist Peter Berger (1963), a sociological perspective grants us the ability to see the foreign in the familiar and the familiar in the foreign. In this chapter we will cover the development of sociology, its various levels of analysis, and sociological research methods, with the intention of elevating our collective consciousness.

⊘ CHAPTER OBJECTIVES

After completing this chapter students should be able to do the following:

- ✔ **Explain** how an understanding of history and biography are essential to igniting the sociological imagination.
- ✔ **Trace** the development of sociology abroad and in the United States.
- ✔ **Discuss** some of foundational figures in the discipline.
- ✔ **Identify** each level of sociological analysis and how each lens can be used to examine aspects of the social world.
- ✔ **Discuss** the basic ideas of social construction, structural-functional, conflict, and symbolic interaction theories.
- ✔ **Explain** the value of sociological research for better understanding the social world.
- ✔ **Explain** the sociological research process and common research methods.
- ✔ **Demonstrate** an understanding of some of the functions of sociological research.

KEY TERMS

sociology	social Darwinism	validity
sociological imagination	theory	qualitative methods
biography	feminist theory	sample
micro level	structural functional theory	symbols
meso level	conflict theory	empirical investigation
macro level	symbolic interaction theory	sympathetic knowledge
theory	positivism	social integration
reliability	quantitative methods	mechanical solidarity
hypothesis	social action	organic solidarity

Sociology is the systematic study of human society. This means that sociologists use scientific methods to explore and interpret the social world. Although research findings are always generalizations, they are more astute than speculation and conjecture. An analysis of the human world includes an understanding of nonhumans like animals, items, and the natural environment, along with an assessment of social arrangements and institutions. A social dissection of society unveils both its glorious and awful elements, and it is important to not overlook either.

As we better understand the social world, we come to better understand ourselves, which may come with some discomfort. However, every shift and change that comes with learning and growing heightens our level of understanding. What is gained from the ability to think critically and to have an elevated social consciousness extends beyond any college class or degree. These qualities remain with you throughout your lives and can be of great benefit as we encounter life's various circumstances.

THE SOCIOLOGICAL IMAGINATION

The word *imagination* is often used to describe fiction or fantasy. As adults acclimate to U.S. culture, we tend to abandon our imagination once we age out of childhood. This is unfortunate because we then restrict our ability to think about alternative realities. What state would our society or world be in if we had not imagined different social arrangements and envisioned more progressive ways of living? Our imagination allows us to expand our thinking and make determinants about our present context and what is possible in the future. The term **sociological imagination** refers to how history shapes the present and the role of external forces in forming our **biography** or personal identities. The book *The Sociological Imagination* was written by Charles Wright Mills (C. Wright Mills) in 1959. According to Mills, in order to "ignite" the sociological imagination, there are a series of critical questions that we must ask ourselves: What is the structure of this particular society? Where does this society stand in human history? In what ways are people selected, formed, liberated, and oppressed? The ability to answer these questions as we assess our society is what Mills (and later Peter Berger) refer to as "the promise" of sociology: A sociological worldview will help us to understand our lives in a larger context. We will more clearly see the various external forces that shape us as individuals and how we as individuals shape our world. We come to realize that our life experience is much more collaborative than we may have thought.

THE DEVELOPMENT OF SOCIOLOGY

Although sociological thought has existed for probably as long as humans have been living and thinking, it took some time for sociology to develop and be recognized as a scientific and academic discipline. It was one of the last of the social sciences to become institutionalized and faced resistance from many governments and intellectuals about its merit and educational value. The history of sociology has often centered European contributions in both persons and place, but sociology has origins all over the world. This chapter will provide a glimpse into some of the more and less known foundational figures in the discipline and the development of sociology in northern Africa (mid–late 1300s), Europe (late 1700s–mid 1800s), the United States (mid–late 1800s), Latin America (late 1800s), East Asia (late 1800s), and South Africa (early 1900s). The oversight and erasure of women and persons of color in the discipline impoverishes sociology, and social science in general, both theoretically and methodologically. Multicultural sources of sociological thought should always be considered as it is what makes the sociological perspective dynamic and comprehensive.

The Founders of Sociology

Although French sociologist **Auguste Comte** (1790–1857) is most commonly credited as the "founder" of sociology, attributed much to his publication of *Positive Philosophy* in 1830, at least two generations of sociologists in the Arab-dominant region of the world have described the work of North African Muslim scholar **Ibn Khaldūn** (1332–1406) as the precursor of modern sociology and considered him "the Arab sociologist of the 14th century" (Alatas, 2014). Khaldūn is not only referenced as the founder of sociology, but the founder of other modern disciplines like philosophy, history, demography, and economics. Ibn Khaldūn has been compared to European sociologists Auguste Comte and Emile Durkheim (1858–1917), both who lived after him but are said to have originated similar ideas. Khaldūn's scholarship focused predominantly on state formation and factors that contribute to their rise and fall. Although his emphasis was on the Ottoman Empire, his theories are applicable to governmental and social structures in our contemporary world.

Both Ibn Khaldūn and Auguste Comte believed it necessary to study history in order to understand the present; both recognized the universality of human nature; both distinguished sociology as a unique discipline, and both recognized the importance of social change. Khaldūn was particularly interested in demonstrative methods such as examining reported events and social conditions as a way to ascertain truth. This perspective is very similar to Comte's notion of **positivism**, which emphasizes objective research through direct observation, experimental design, and comparative analysis.

British sociologist **Harriet Martineau** was writing sociology as early as 1834 drafting what would become her major statement on a scientific method *How to Observe Morals and Manners* (1838). Her scientific method was tested in her classic study *Society in America* (1836). Martineau's is perhaps most well known for her 1853 translation and abridgement of Comte's *Positive Philosophy*. Martineau wrote successfully across a range of disciplines, including literature, political commentary, children's literature, and history.

Martineau felt a conviction to use her talent in writing to serve society:

> I believe myself possessed of no uncommon talents, and of not an atom of genius; but as various circumstances have led me to think more accurately and read more extensively than some women, I believe that I may so write on subjects of universal concern as to inform some minds and stir up others. (Martineau, 1877, III33, as cited in Lengermann and Niebrugge, 2007, p. 23)

Sociologist Aldon D. Morris opens his book *The Scholar Denied: W.E.B DuBois and the Birth of Modern Sociology* (2015), with the following statement:

> There is an intriguing, well-kept secret regarding the founding of scientific sociology in America. The first school of scientific sociology in the United States was founded by a Black professor located in a historically Black university in the South. This reality flatly contradicts the accepted wisdom. (p. 1)

William Edward Burghardt (W.E.B) DuBois (1868–1963) developed and operated the first applied sociology school in the United States called the Atlanta Sociological Laboratory, from 1895–1924. According to DuBois, the "emerging social sciences should be built on careful, empirical research focused on human action in order to pass the test as genuine science" (Morris, 2015, p. 3). Where much sociological research in the United States had relied on conjecture and speculation, DuBois established a sociological laboratory for systemic empirical research in that hypotheses could be accepted or rejected based on data collection through scientific methods. One of DuBois's early investigative studies focused on the Black American community of Philadelphia, *The Philadelphia Negro* (1900). DuBois's research challenged dominant racist views of the 20th century as well as the scientific racism that supported the oppression of Black and Indigenous people. The failure to acknowledge DuBois's scholarship and his role in pioneering empirical research is evidence of the upholding of notions of Eurocentric authority and superiority.

Sociology in Europe

The French Revolution that began in 1789 continuing for the next 10 years was galvanizing for sociological analysis. A combination of rapid population growth, struggles for political control, and economic depression led to social unrest and violent revolts. At the same time, the industrial revolution was underway in Great Britain and Ireland, drastically transforming modes of work and social and economic arrangements. Much of the contention during this period focused on the power and resources held by the elite in an emerging capitalist system. English sociologist **Herbert Spencer** (1820–1903) received much acclaim for his Darwinian-influenced ideas about natural selection, coining the term **social Darwinism**; he argued that people and patterns that were "fit" would survive and those that were "unfit" would die out. Spencer argued that governments should not interfere with the natural processes of society, as humans would progressively adapt to their environment and reach higher levels of development. For some this was justification for unrestrained capitalism. (Hughes & Kroehler, 2007).

German-born **Karl Marx** (1818–1883) was not specifically a sociologist but contributed to sociological thought through his expertise in the areas of history, economics, philosophy, and political science. Much of Marx's work focused on economic environments in which societies develop. He was particularly interested in methods of production, the division of labor, and class conflict. According to Marx, all economic orders reach maximum efficiency and then internal weaknesses lead to their decline. Marx believed that capitalism would eventually be replaced with socialism, and socialism by communism, which he asserted was the highest stage of society (Marx, 1906). Although Marx's ideas have not reached fruition, his theoretical perspectives and contributions to the study of capitalism remain important in modern social analysis.

Contrary to Marx's focus on class divisions in society, French sociologist **Emile Durkheim** (1858–1918) focused on how societies form solidarity and endure during times of conflict and transformation. Like Marx, Durkheim was also interested in the industrial revolution's impact on the division of labor, but particularly on how it impacted social ties. Central to Durkheim's sociological perspective was **social integration**, the density or number of relationships among a collective. He believed that the more people were connected, the stronger and more meaningful relationships would be. Durkheim argued that the nature of solidarity had shifted with the onset of the industrial revolution, from **mechanical solidarity**, a society with a simple division of labor in which shared knowledge bestows common experiences and beliefs, to **organic solidarity**, a social system in which people are known by one another based on their specialized roles in the labor structure. Durkheim's observations of mechanical and organic solidarity mirrored those of German sociologist **Ferdinand Tönnies** (1855–1936), who distinguished between two types of social groups using the terms *gemeinschaft*, referring to social ties that were community based and established through personal interactions and shared beliefs, versus *gesellschaft*, which are social ties based on indirect interaction, formal values, and impersonal social roles.

Another German sociologist and contemporary of Durkheim was **Max Weber** (1864–1920). Weber wrote about Tönnies's concepts of *gemeinschaft* and *gesellschaft* as key elements of historical and social change. Weber used the term **social action** to refer to the actions people take both in response to others and with motivation from larger forces and settings. Weber was also interested in human subjectivity, the intentions and beliefs that underlie people's behavior. While Marx felt that capitalism was a driving force for social change, Weber believed that religion played a larger role in shaping people's behavior.

Max Weber's wife **Marianne Weber** (1870–1954) should also be recognized for her contributions to the discipline of sociology. After her husband's death, she edited and published 10 volumes of his work and wrote a biography of him. Marianne Weber debated the ideas of both her husband and Georg Simmel in her own writings, which include eight books of social analysis and sociology. During her lifetime, Marianne Weber was recognized a feminist intellectual, a sociologist of law, and a social theorist. Weber's sociological investigation is grounded in a critical feminist analysis that centers women's issues and perspectives. One of her major works, *Authority and Autonomy in Marriage* (1912), provides a historical and structural analysis of marriage and women's rights within the institution. In the text she explores micro-level dynamics of marriage such as ongoing negotiation over power and intimacy, women's work, and sexuality. Weber's insertion of feminism into a male-dominated sociological discourse helped to develop a new kind of sociology and more critical sociology than had previously existed (Lengermann & Niebrugge, 2007).

Sociology in the United States

Anna Julia Cooper (1858–1964) and **Ida B. Wells-Burnett** (1862–1931) both knew and worked with sociologist W.E.B DuBois. Cooper and Wells-Burnett formed a non-Marxian conflict theory that addressed the Black American experience within a Black feminist framework. In the early 1890s, each of the women published significant sociological works: Cooper, a collection of essays titled *A Voice from the South* (1892) and Wells-Burnett, two research pamphlets, *Southern Horrors* (1892) and *A Red Record* (1895). The American Civil War and the following period of Reconstruction heavily shaped and patterned the lives of Cooper and Wells-Burnett. Their White women peers in sociology could choose to go into difficult situations, examine them, and retreat to a place of physical and material comfort, whereas Cooper and Wells-Burnett lived and endured persistent racism and discrimination. Cooper and Wells-Burnett, along with another leading figure in the Black women's movement, Mary Church Terrell, expressed their perspectives and experiences in double and triple contexts: "as Blacks and as women to White Americans, as women to Black men, and as individuals of particular class backgrounds to and for themselves" (Lengermann & Neibrugge, 2007, pp. 159–160). These women constructed a sociological analysis of U.S. society that focused on power and difference. Their multidimensional lens of race, gender, and class helped to generate a Black feminist sociology. Like Harriet Martineau, these women followed a methodological practice that accounted for the particular biography of women with intersecting variables such as history, race, religion, nationality, and social class.

Jane Addams (1860–1935) was the founder of Hull-House, a famous Chicago social settlement and major research institution. Addams identified herself as a sociologist, taught sociology, and was a member of the American Sociological Association (called the American Sociological Society until 1959). She was a spokesperson for progressive social reform on behalf of women, immigrants, children, trade unions, Black Americans, and working-class people. Like Cooper and Wells-Burnett, Addams formulated a research methodology that centered various vantage points. One of Addams's major theoretical contributions were her essays included in a multivolume of critical research and theory by Hull-House residents called *The Hulls-House Maps and Papers, by Residents of Hull-House: A Presentation of Nationalities and Wages in a Congested District of Chicago, Together with Comments and Essays on Problems Growing out of Social Conditions* (1895). Addams employed a method that can be called **sympathetic knowledge** or sympathetic observation that values the knowledge and experiences of those being studied and considers them co-collaborators in the research process. Additionally, Addams felt that a purpose and responsibility to not only study marginalized individuals and social problems, but to develop ways to ameliorate them.

The **Chicago School** refers to a group of sociologists who influenced the development of sociology as an academic discipline in the early 20th century. The Chicago School was established in 1892 with the first department of sociology in the United States and was the primary institute of sociology study between 1915 and 1935. A number of sociologists carried out research on immigrant ghettos, juvenile gangs, mental illness, prostitution, and wealth disparities. A few influential figures include Edward Franklin Frazier, Edith and Grace Abbott, George Herbert Mead, Sophonisba Breckinridge, W.I. Thomas, and Florence Kelley. We will revisit the contributions of many of these individuals in subsequent chapters. The work carried out by Chicago school sociologists remains influential in the field of sociology today.

Sociology in Latin America

Latin America is a vast land, more than twice the size of Europe, including Russia, with about 20 nation-states and a population of over 642 million people. In the 1860s sociological studies became separate from other disciplines. Sociology was, and remains today, linked with the study of law in Latin American universities. The onset of sociology tended to resemble an anthropological examination of native groups and community organization. Latin America has had a large number of *mestizo* or ethnically mixed individuals, and while this did not create the severity of racial conflict that occurred in places like the United States, the existence of various ethnic groups living side by side did present its share of challenges. European **colonization**, the takeover of land and people by a foreign group, the enslavement of Africans, independence, the importation of modern ideas, the emancipation of slaves, and a number of economic, social, and political entanglements between the United States and Latin America presented much for Latin American social scientists to study and investigate. Domingo F. Sarmiento (1811–1888) is regarded as the first Latin Americas sociologist. In his publication *Facundo* (1854) Sarmiento argues that South America was faced with "a constant struggle between civilization and barbarism" (Gisbert, 1952, p. 128). Another pioneer of sociology in Latin America, also Argentinian, was Juan B. Alberdi (1810–1884). Much of Alberdi's writings were social-political, directed toward government critique. In one of his first books, *El voto de America* (*The Vow of America*, 1835), he heavily criticized President Monroe's Pan-American doctrine.

The early Latin American approach to social inquiry was much more historical and political than sociological, as it lacked a sociological method. This was in part due to the following of European models of the time and in part due to the struggle between positivism and pragmatism. However, sociology has undergone another round of development in contemporary times, and a new Latin American sociology has been forged by pioneering figures: Gino Germani in Argentina, Pablo González Casanova in Mexico, and Fernando Hernrique Cardoso in Brazil (Smith, 1988).

Sociology in East Asia

East Asia refers to specifically mainland China, Taiwan, Hong Kong, Japan, and South Korea. The emergence and development of sociology in East Asia was influenced by a variety of regional and global as well as national and local forces. Some of the global factors include colonization, the Cold War, and communism. A few of the national and local forces include cultural heritage and historical legacy.

The first department of sociology was established in Japan at the University of Tokyo (formerly Tokyo Imperial University) in 1893. Unlike its East Asian counterparts, sociology in Japan is firmly established and institutionalized. The Japan Sociological Society (JSS) is the second largest sociological association in the world, with more than 3,700 members. St. John's University in Shanghai, China, offered sociology courses taught by American missionaries in 1914. However, sociology was banned in mainland China after the 1949 Communist Revolution and did not re-emerge until 1979. China's Communist Party state and robust economy provided conditions favorable to the expansion of sociology by providing funding for various research initiatives (So, 2015).

The development of sociology in Taiwan is unique compared to other East Asian nations in that it has focused on an Indigenous-centered sociology. A new generation of sociologists who were born in China but grew up in Taiwan rejected American models and theories because they did not fit the nature of Taiwanese society. The Japanese colonization of the divide between Taiwan and mainland China has brought about a critical analysis and resistance in the direction and scholarship of Taiwanese sociologists. In line with the "Indigenization" effort began in the 1980s, the Taiwanese Sociological Association was formed in 1995. In the 21st century Taiwan has a diverse, engaged, and vibrant sociology that aspires to be both Indigenous and international. This is the contemporary approach to East Asian sociology in general, to be more reflexive, and gain more international recognition (So, 2015).

Sociology in South Africa

South African apartheid had a major influence of the emergence and stagnant development of sociology in this region. According to Michael Buraway (2004, p. 15, as cited in Webster, 2004), "The post-apartheid state ... has little patience for public and critical sociologies that articulate the disparate interests to be found in society. The assault on sociology becomes part of a broader offensive against active society" (p. 27).

The early stages of South African sociology focused on legitimating a range of activities that were not normally accepted as professional or academic. Sociology departments in South Africa developed as a part of social world programs with a strong emphasis on public policy. The first department of sociology and social work in South Africa was established at the University of Pretoria in the 1920s. In the late 1950s Talcott Parson's structural functionalism was introduced into South African sociology. This perspective provided South African sociology with a unique theoretical framework, which led to its break from social work in the 1960s.

The Association for Sociology in Southern Africa (ASSA) was formed in 1971, but Black sociologists were not allowed into the organization until 1977. During the 1980s, the ASSA were in close dialogue with social movements struggling against apartheid. The engaged nature of sociological studies brought about alternative organizations and publications. There were a variety of dilemmas that faced sociologists engaging in the field. According to Edward Webster (2004), valuable lessons were drawn from the critical engagement of university sociologists and general members of South African society:

- Public sociologists have to recognize that society has its own organic intellectuals, and in intervening, they will either reinforce or subvert existing power relations within society.
- The successful practice of public sociology depends on a strong professional sociology located in a university with a clear commitment to the autonomy of the researcher.
- The public sociologist wields influence not power.
- The production of knowledge is a contested process, and one cannot ignore the disciplinary foundations of the production process.

With the end of formal apartheid in South Africa, institutional changes took place that placed less focus on social movements and the democratization process but centered the more policy-oriented research demands of the state. Today, many South African sociologists are active in the International Sociological Association (ISA). The ISA now has a working group to study ways of promoting recognition of sociological research work carried out in Africa, Asia, and Latin America. We will conclude this section with words from one of their documents:

> The field of sociology has, for historical reasons, been widely defined in Europe and North America, and often reflects the problems, cultural models, modes of access, production and diffusion of knowledge of Western countries or countries where Western intellectual traditions dominate. Social issues specific to non-Western cultures or developing countries have frequently been marginalized or ignored. Major sociological communities in Latin America or Asia still find it difficult to situate their research concerns and their theoretical developments not only within the framework and discussion of general theories that the West has universalized, but also in international sociological conferences and world congresses. We all know the role major Western philosophical traditions and social science theories have played in the diversification of sociological discourse. Wider access to work from the (global) South or from Asia would also considerably enrich the perspectives of the discipline. (Webster & Fakier, 2001, pp. 26–27, as cited in Webster 2004, p. 39).

LEVELS OF ANALYSIS

A sociological worldview provides multiple lens for examining society. There are three general levels of sociological analysis: the *macro level*, *meso level*, and *micro level*. The macro level is the broadest level of society. With a **macro-level analysis**, we look at far-reaching aspects of the social world such as international trends, whole nations, and global forces. A **meso-level analysis**, or intermediate level of analysis, focuses on formal institutions and organizations that bring people together. These institutions and organizations are of a smaller scale than entire nations but larger than a local community. They are nationwide in range. A meso-level analysis can also include ethnic groups that share a group identity because they are too large to know each individual but small enough to be able to become familiar with some of their characteristics. A **micro-level analysis** examines small-scale and typically face-to-face interactions in small groups. Micro-level interaction is the foundation of all social groups, organizations, and institutions.

These three levels of analysis are not independent of one another. We can think of the interplay of these levels by recalling the earthquake that hit Haiti on January 12, 2010. At the macro level, the disaster initiated relief efforts around the world and had an impact on the international economic exchange. At the meso level, the earthquake obviously changed the lives of Haitians by physically displacing about 5 million people and damaging or destroying nearly 4,000 schools. At the micro level, individuals and families were faced with the abrupt death of loved ones and loss of belongings, along with an emerging cholera outbreak (Reid, 2019).

Applying Sociology: Macro, Meso, Micro

Think about the various parts of Education on a macro, meso, and micro level. Identify three possible units (institutions, organizations, groups, individuals) at each level of analysis.

The micro (college) level:

1. _____

2. _____

3. _____

The meso (state, organizational) level:

1. _____

2. _____

3. _____

The micro (small group, individual student) level:

1. _____

2. _____

3. _____

Source: Adapted from Ballantine and Roberts (2012).

MAJOR THEORETICAL PERSPECTIVES

Although the word **theory** sounds extremely academic, people theorize all the time. We are constantly asking ourselves (and others) why certain things happen and making predictions about future behavior and occurrences. In sociology, there are core theories that we use to guide our **empirical investigation** of social life. Empirical investigation involves the collection and analysis of data, theoretical guidance, and an assessment of information. Theories provide a framework for understanding by identifying specific areas of focus and the use of informed assertions. Most of the core sociological theories, such as the **structural-functional theory**, **conflict theory**, and **feminist theory**, are macro-level theories that focus on large-scale social phenomena. The **symbolic interaction theory** is the only micro-level theory of the four discussed in this chapter. Each of these sociological theories examine the socially created nature of social life, otherwise known as *social construction*. The social construction perspective does not completely remove the role of an individual's free will to act. However, sociologists, as objective-oriented scientists, regard the external influences of the social world, such as the process of learning and cultural indoctrination, as significant contributors to both individual and collective behavior.

Structural-Functional Theory

The structural-functional, or functionalist, theory focuses on social order and stability. Functional theorists believe that all parts of the social structure contribute to the overall ability of a society to maintain itself and function in particular ways. It is also important to examine dysfunctional aspects of society that undermine its stability. Both function and dysfunction in parts of society highlight important elements of the social structure.

Theory	Applied Example	Sociologists Aligned with Theory
Structural-functional	Sociologists thinking from a *structural-functional* perspective would view the COVID-19 pandemic as a major disruption to social order and function. They would highlight the strengths and weaknesses of various social institutions and structures charged with responding to the outbreak and caring for members of the society.	Herbert Spencer, Emile Durkheim

FIGURE 1.1 *Structural-functional theory applied to COVID-19 pandemic.*

Conflict Theory

The conflict theory contends that inequality and injustice are major sources of conflict that permeate society. Conflict theorists highlight group competition for resources and the powerful decision-makers who impose their values and beliefs on the rest of society. While structural-functional theorists hold that each part of society has a role in establishing balance and equilibrium, conflict theorists underscore the maintenance of social order by domination and exploitation by governing members of society.

Theory	Applied Example	Sociologists Aligned With Theory
Conflict	Those drawing from *conflict theory* would think about the privilege of those with health insurance and jobs capable of operating during quarantine. They would also examine the interests of those in power to determine the measures needed to address the crisis.	Ida B. Wells-Burnett, Karl Marx

FIGURE 1.2 *Conflict theory applied to COVID-19 pandemic.*

Feminist Theory

As previously discussed, much of the history of sociology has erased the contributions of women sociologists who offered a significant gender analysis to the discipline. However, gradually these women are being recognized, and even more, mainstream society is having conversations about gender dynamics and inequities. Feminist theory emphasizes the ways gender differences are socially constructed and used to justify and maintain gender inequity. While feminist theory is closely linked to conflict theory, feminist theorists emphasize that women and feminine-presenting individuals are disadvantaged by the hierarchical power arrangement of society, whereas men experience privilege due to those same arrangements.

Theory	Applied Example	Sociologists Aligned With Theory
Feminist	A thinker inspired by *feminist theory* would recognize the necessary reorganization of standard gender roles required to live and work in quarantine. They would take note of reduced emphasis on gendered behavior and expression due to the focus on stability and survival.	Harriet Martineau, Anna Julia Cooper

FIGURE 1.3 *Feminist theory applied to COVID-19 pandemic.*

Symbolic Interaction Theory

Symbolic interaction theory examines everyday interactions and communications between people derived from **symbols**, which are things to which we attach meaning. Furthermore, symbols are typically objects that we assign a name or value, but people also carry symbolic meaning. Symbolic interactionists are interested in how shared meaning is developed and the system of behavioral expectations it brings forth.

Theory	Applied Example	Sociologists Aligned With Theory
Symbolic interaction	Sociologists using the *symbolic interaction* framework reflect on the symbols and messaging around the COVID-19 pandemic. Their thoughts extend to the ways that people redefine their reality in quarantine and the normalization of things like wearing face masks.	George Herbert Mead, Max Weber

FIGURE 1.4 *Symbolic interaction theory applied to COVID-19 pandemic.*

SOCIOLOGICAL RESEARCH

While there is some value to using "common sense," it should not replace formal research as we seek to better understand ourselves and the world. In Auguste Comte's conception of **positivism**, he encouraged social scientists to reject personal opinions and to be as objective as possible in their analysis. At the Atlanta Sociological Laboratory, W.E.B. Dubois held the belief that research benefits from collaboration and the use of multiple methodologies. As humans we have inherent biases, but scientific research is structured in a way that considers this problem at the start and provides steps and strategies for reducing or interrupting personal prejudices. Both educational research and popular media reveals to us that people think about things in a variety of different ways based on personal and social factors. What is considered standard to some is uncommon to others. In this section we will examine a general sociological research model; however, some studies omit or alter certain steps.

A Research Model
Step 1: Identify of a Topic or Issue

This step may seem obvious and not worth stating, but it is important to take careful consideration when determining a research objective. A research topic should be clearly defined, and the researcher should know whether they are striving to answer a question that lacks information or whether they are attempting to fill a gap in our understanding. It is impossible to collect data from an entire population, so researchers must narrow their focus to a specific **sample**, or individuals intended to represent the population to be studied.

Step 2: Review Existing Information

It is of little value to carry out research on a topic that has been thoroughly examined with generally satisfactory conclusions. It is important to learn what has already been published or known about a topic and decide what your contribution could be. Reviewing the existing literature can also help guide your specific questions that need to be addressed or areas that have not been examined. Drawing from other's ideas and information can also help to identify appropriate research methods.

Step 3: Define the Issue

A literature review should help a researcher to define their topic of study more clearly. At this stage, a **hypothesis**, a statement of how variables are expected to be related to one another, can be formed. This may also lead to the development of a particular theoretical framework to guide your research. Before moving forward, researchers should know exactly what they hope to learn about the topic.

Step 4: Choose a Research Method

The fourth step in this process is determining how to collect data on your topic. There are several different research methods possible, but there may be only a few that are suited for your research topic and objective. You will also want to select a research method that allows you to answer your study's specific questions.

Step 5: Collect Data

In this step you carry out the research using the selected research method. This process may not always move smoothly, and it may be necessary to rethink the initial strategy. When engaging with human participants it is possible to face refusal to answer questions or to be denied access to important records. However, it may be necessary to obtain this information for **validity**, or extent that you are measuring what is intended to be measured. In this case adopting a different approach will enhance the **reliability**, or likelihood for consistent, dependable results.

Step 6: Interpret Results

After the completion of data collection begins another major step in the research process: analyzing the results. If a hypothesis or theory was part of the research study, your results will allow you to test them. This is another aspect of the research process that requires clarity and a summation of the research intentions.

Step 7: Report the Findings

The conclusion of your research involves sharing your findings with the scientific and/or public community. A research report provides an account of your research objective, research method, findings, and the significance of the findings for additional understanding of the topic. There can be a comparison and contrast of existing work on the topic if applicable, and new or unanswered questions could be suggested for future study.

Research Methods

We will now review some of the research methods that sociologists use keeping in mind that the research method one chooses is largely shaped by the questions posed in the research study. **Qualitative methods** are approaches that tend to rely on personal and collective accounts or observations of a person or situation. These methods render open-ended data that may require more interpretation but provide a deeper meaning of the subject matter. **Quantitative methods** render data that is more objective and statistical. The data drawn from quantitative methods can account for trends, enable comparisons, or reveal correlations. A mixed-method approach is common for modern social scientists as it allows flexible research and multifaceted results and analysis.

Research Method	Implementation	Advantages	Challenges
Survey	– Interviews – Questionnaires	– Ability to survey a large sample – Yields numerous responses	– Time-consuming – Must encourage participant participation – May not accurately capture how people think and behave in real life
Participant Observation/ fieldwork	– Observation – Ethnography – Case studies	– Provides detailed, more accurate, real-life information	– Time consuming – May not capture what people think and believe
Experiments	Manipulation of a setting or materials to determine cause and effect	– Establishes clear cause and effect relationship	– May raise ethical concerns – Participants may be inclined to alter their behavior
Secondary data analysis	Examination of documents such as records, books, and governmental data	– Makes use and takes account of previous information on a topic	– The objective of previous research may differ from your own – Some data may be hard to find or limited

Source: Adapted from Salituro (2020).

Emile Durkheim and a Secondary Data Analysis of Suicide

Emile Durkheim's book *Suicide* (1897/1951) was a landmark study in sociology as he was presumably the first to document suicide as a manifestation of changes in society as opposed to psychological troubles. Durkheim developed a theory that the structure of society could determine suicide rates. He utilized secondary data analysis by comparing existing official statistics and historical records across groups. Over a span of about 7 years Durkheim examined the available data on suicide rates in Europe: across different regions of countries, by certain religious and ethnic groups, by marital status, and so forth, looking for social patterns.

Durkheim concluded by identifying several types of suicide. He also found that suicide rates in all countries examined were higher among single, widowed, and divorced people than married people; higher among people without children than parents; and higher among Protestants than among Catholics. Durkheim felt that it was the nature of social life among people in these groups that increased the likelihood of suicide. Durkheim's research challenged the idea that suicide was purely based on individual factors but instead a result of the evolution of social arrangements, meanings, and expectations.

The Limitations and Possibilities of Sociological Research

Sociological research can provide a wealth of understanding and answers about nearly all social phenomena. However, research does not always provide (or seek to provide) solutions to social problems. It is likely that a thorough study of sociological and social science research can guide one in the direction of a variety of solutions to social problems, but we should not think of this as its ultimate duty. Many of the founding figures of sociology engaged in research for the purpose of finding solutions to society's plights, and sociology departments historically and presently are closely linked to social work, a public-facing, solution-driven field. But reform is not the goal of all sociologists, and people should not set out with this expectation. Research cannot be considered the only tool for addressing social change. Regardless of how thorough it may be, research has limitations. Research results will always be generalizations no matter how many people are sampled. We can never completely know how each person on the earth lives or thinks. It is impossible to completely rid ourselves of personal biases that shape our outlook and initiatives, let alone the overwhelming hierarchies and stratification of the larger social structure. Change involves not only the way that we think and act, but also the transformation of structures and arrangements in society. Sociology should be used as a powerful resource for understanding the world and its people, but ultimately it is the people themselves who have the capacity to make transformative changes.

SUMMARY: CONNECTING THE PIECES

A sociological worldview involves igniting a sociological imagination that will provide a broad context in which to view the world. Historical assessment is critical for developing a sociological perspective. Our biographical stories are part of the shaping of history, and history shapes our personal stories. The promise of sociology is that you will see the world and its people in new ways. Examining society through various levels of analysis with the guidance of theoretical perspectives and rigorous scientific research is how sociologists have come to understand society as a social system with interdependent parts. Academic sociology evolved as societies around the world were adjusting to political, social, and economic changes. Early sociological research was a great resource for intellectual development and social justice initiatives. Although sociology does not provide a blueprint for solving all of the world's problems, it can help us to better see and understand the world, thus becoming more conscious humans with the potential to effect positive social change.

REVIEW AND CRITICAL THINKING

Directions: Respond to the questions and prompts based on what you have learned in this chapter:

1. How is the sociological imagination connected to "the promise" of sociology?
2. How are micro, meso, and macro levels of analyses connected?
3. What makes sociology a science?
4. Compare and contrast the development of sociology around the world.
5. Connect one or more of the foundational figures in sociology to a major theoretical perspective.
6. Describe the sociological research process.
7. Discuss the post-research considerations and limitations to research.

Credit

IMG 1.1: Gordon Parks, https://commons.wikimedia.org/wiki/File:Paul_Robeson_1942_crop.jpg, Office of War Information, 1942.

CHAPTER 2

Culture(s)

Today, the most noticeable impact of President Nixon's 1971 proclamation "the war on drugs" are the nearly 2 million individuals who are currently incarcerated and the hundreds of thousands who are under law enforcement supervision (i.e., probation, parole) due to low-level drug offenses. The decade of the 1960s in America is remembered as a turbulent period of social unrest, political assassinations, and heightened drug use. It was also a time of progressive social movements and civil and human rights legislation. Younger generations may be less familiar with the censorship and sanctioning of music that presumably promoted recreational drug use during this time. Throughout the 1960s and 70s, so-called "drug songs" would be a key target on the war on drugs battlefront. The Federal Bureau of Narcotics (1930–1968) engaged in long propaganda campaigns transmitting erroneous information about the use and impact of drugs, namely marijuana. Films like *Marijuana: Weeds with Roots in Hell*, *Devil's Harvest*, and *Reefer Madness* promoted in the 1930s were effective in alarming many Americans as well as racializing drug use.

Image 2.1

Peter, Paul, and Mary's 1963 classic "Puff the Magic Dragon" was viewed by America's drug warriors as an ode to marijuana consumption. Critiques equated "puff" with marijuana, "dragon" as code for inhaling, and "mists" as clouds of exhaled smoke. A song that had once been viewed as childlike and benign became a nefarious anthem for drug use (Blecha, 2004).

The Drug Policy Alliance, established in 2000, estimates that the United States spends $51 billion annually on antidrug initiatives, but more than 14,500 specialized drug treatment facilities lack or have insufficient coverage for substance abuse treatment (National Institutes of Health [NIH], 2017). A sociological perspective would also draw our attention to the bias and hypocrisy of drug narratives in the United States. Although many songs reference drugs and drug use, focus is disproportionately given to hip hop and rock and roll music. Furthermore, some of the most addictive and life-threatening drugs, such as alcohol and tobacco, are not only legal, but often celebrated and promoted through American media. The term *overprescription* has emerged and refers to the overprescribing of particularly addictive drugs by medical professionals. Drug narratives, laws, and policies are not purely based on concerns regarding public health, they are also derived from strong social and political interests.

✓ CHAPTER OBJECTIVES

After completing this chapter students should be able to do the following:

✔ **Define** culture and its function in society.

✔ **Describe** the key components of culture.

✔ **Explain** cultural diversity and cultural differences.

✔ **Explain** the relationship between material and nonmaterial culture.

✔ **Discuss** how culture is transmitted throughout history, by individuals and groups, and through social institutions.

✔ **Recognize** the role of youth in shaping popular culture.

✔ **Discuss** some of the strategies used for inclusive and progressive cultural change.

KEY TERMS

Culture
Nonmaterial culture
Material culture
Symbols
Norms
Language
Beliefs
Values

Formal sanctions
Informal sanctions
Mores
Cultural diversity
Subculture
Counterculture
Cultural capital
Cultural relativism

Cultural reproduction
Ethnocentrism

Most sociologists would agree that culture is a key element that differentiates societies around the world. **Culture** can be defined as the language, values, beliefs, norms, customs, and material objects that characterize a society. Cultural ideas and items are reproduced by their transmission from one generation to the next. Social institutions, organizations, and groups provide the framework for culture, which in turn provides guidelines for living. Due to the generally unnoticed nature of culture, it is only recognized when there is a dramatic social change, a mass crisis, or circumstances lead us to compare ourselves or our society to another.

On a macro level, we are products of the historical period in which we live. On a meso level, we embody the cultural ideas and customs of our geographic location in the world. At the micro level, we are shaped by the specific cultural influences of our communities and social groups. Although culture produces a distinctive character for each society, cultural elements are exchanged worldwide. The task of the sociologist is to understand cultural diversity by examining societies by their own standards, otherwise known as **cultural relativism**. Cultural relativism acts as a check against the idealism of one's home culture by examining ideas and behaviors in specific cultural contexts.

CONSTRUCTING REALITY

It has been said that what distinguishes humans from animals is that humans have a complex language system and broad cognitive capacity. Humans have constructed a social reality through the physical development of social structures using land and natural resources and the conceptual development of assigned labels and meanings. The combination of material and nonmaterial culture forms a sophisticated social system in which millions (billions worldwide) of people are able to coexist and evolve. **Material culture** consists of the physical objects that individuals develop. Material culture includes things such as food, clothes, cars, tools, and technologies. Material items have symbolic meaning for humans as well. **Symbols** are literally expressed in speech and writing, but they also provide meaning and associations that aid our understanding and communication. Philosopher Susanne Langer asserted that using symbols to construct reality lies at the heart of what makes us human. Since words are important in constructing reality, the following passage from Langer is edited to include gender-neutral pronouns:

> Only as small part of reality, for human beings is what is actually going on; the greater part is what they imagine in connection with the sights and sounds of the moment ... It means that their world is bigger than the stimuli which surround them, and the measure of it is the reach of their coherent and steady imagination. An animal's environment consists of the things that act on the senses. ... Animals do not live in a world of unbroken space and time, filled with events even when they are not present or when they are not interested; their "world" has a fragmentary, intermittent existence, arising and collapsing

with their activities. A human being's world hangs together, its events fit into each other; no matter how devious their connections, there always are connections, in one big framework of time and space. ... *The world* is something human (Langer, 1962, as cited in Johnson, 2014, p. 31)

We will explore the significance of language in shaping culture and our social world more in the next section, but it is clear that words help to make things *real*. Language has the power to construct realities that cannot be achieved through our senses alone. Language and symbols are examples of **nonmaterial culture**, the invisible and intangible parts of a culture. Along with language and symbols, nonmaterial culture includes beliefs, values, and social norms. Material items in a society can reveal a lot about the nonmaterial culture of a society. For example, portable and reusable drink containers are common in U.S. culture. These material items symbolize cultural values associated with conservation and sustainability. They also communicate information about the nature of life in the United States, where most people are often traveling and spending significant amounts of time away from their homes.

Culture and society are not independent of one another. They are inextricably connected as culture is the adhesive that connects the multiple facets of society. What takes place in each part of society is informed by cultural guidelines.

COMPONENTS OF CULTURE

While the essence of culture is complex, we can better understand it by exploring its key components. In the previous section we saw that symbols and language were significant elements of culture. Here, we will briefly revisit language, following an examination of the construction and use of cultural beliefs, values, and norms.

Language

One could argue that language is really the key to culture because it is what facilitates its transmission. Language encompasses the accumulated knowledge of centuries of symbols that have granted people the ability to communicate with one another. Beyond spoken language, there are also numerous forms of written language in the form of alphabets, scripts, and characters. For people like Helen Keller (1880–1968), who was blind and deaf due to an illness in infancy, the ability to communicate through traditional speech was not an option. Sign language turned out to be the mechanism to end Keller's isolation and lead her to becoming a renowned educator (Macionis, 2008). Although sign language has as visual-manual component, it also includes nonmanual elements such as postures and movements of body, head, eyebrow, eyes, cheeks, and mouth. This nonverbal communication can be used to convey verbs of emotion, questions, and negation. Most humans use a combination of verbal and nonverbal communication in our interactions with one another.

Image 2.2

However, we would not be able to effectively communicate without first establishing what these symbols mean through shared beliefs and values.

The *symbolic interaction perspective* would draw our attention to the ways that we use language to express our views and sense of self. The women in the image wearing simple white shirts with black text use powerful words without speaking. The lack of any stylization or design draws even more attention to the powerful words they wear. The woman on the left's slogan reminds us that, not long ago, women were effectively silent when it came to rights like voting and divorce, a stark reminder that such rights are even now under fire. The individual on the right, in contrast, wears an optimistic slogan, proclaiming woman will have an impactful place in the future. Wearing such bold statements can be an effective tool to empower oneself.

Nowadays, we are walking advertisements for corporations and businesses by wearing their names on our clothing and accessories. In the last several years of political protests and justice movements in the United States, it has

Image 2.3

Image 2.4

become commonplace to see T-shirts stating one's views on certain issues or making particular proclamations. Individuals have used this type of messaging as a form of empowerment and a tool for activism.

The *structural-functional perspective* highlights the ways a shared dominant language contributes to the order and stability of society. According to the U.S. Census Bureau (2015), there are at least 350 languages spoken in U.S. homes. Withstanding such linguistic variation, members of society can still effectively communicate because there is a cultural understanding (and expectation) that English be used as the primary language. As an already ethnically diverse society has become even more multicultural, public information and documents are increasingly available in a variety of different languages.

The *conflict perspective* directs our attention to how language is used to promote ideas about social unity and interdependency, concealing the fact that there are significant economic imbalances and centralized power relations among members of U.S. society. Social crises currently and historically have disproportionately impacted individuals with less economic affluence, less education, and less social prestige.

Gendered Language	Neutral Language
Girls and boys, you guys	Students, pupils, scholars, kiddos, children, people, friends
Mommies and daddies	Grown-ups, adults, families
Husband, wife, girlfriend, boyfriend	Partner, spouse

Laurin Mayeno Consulting, http://www.mayenoconsulting.com/wordpress/using-gender-inclusive-language-with-children-families-7-tips/. Copyright © 2018 by Laurin Mayeno Consulting.

The *feminist perspective* points out the gendered nature of language and the ways language is used to reinforce male or masculine dominance and authority. Gender equity advocates have encouraged the use of gender-neutral terminology, recognizing that gendered language is not needed in most situations but is used to maintain and perpetuate inequalities.

Beliefs and Values

It is apparent that the way that we think informs the way that we act. Every culture determines what is true or false, appropriate, or inappropriate, important or insignificant, through the establishment of beliefs and values. Sociologist W. I. Thomas and his wife Dorothy Swain Thomas (1928) made the classic assertion that if we define a situation as real then it is real in its consequences. Robert K. Merton (1976) went further to state that what is real has consequences whether it is defined as real or not. It is sometimes a challenge to determine what is "real" or not in the world of social media, claims of "fake news," and scripted reality television. Although many individuals hold their personal beliefs to be irrefutable facts, beliefs are indeed cultural and vary by group, region, and historical period. **Beliefs** can be defined as ideas about what people consider to be true or false. **Values** are standards used to decide what is socially desirable, good or bad, superior and inferior. Values are broad and at times abstract, whereas beliefs tend to be specific. Values reinforce or undermine particular beliefs. For example, a country that values democratic principles would establish belief systems that support educational access and equal opportunities for all its members. While *ideal* culture is not always *real*, lived culture, moral standards, are important, nonetheless.

Norms

Beliefs and values assist in the development of **norms**, which are rules and expectations that guide behavior in a society. Unlike beliefs and values, norms that have great moral significance, otherwise known as **mores**, apply throughout a society at all times. For instance, there is widespread aversion in U.S. society toward adults engaging in sexual relations with children. While individuals may not abide by every social norm, most people do conform to them due to the **formal sanctions**, norms backed by laws, rules, or policies, or the **informal sanctions**, unofficial expressions of approval or disapproval that may result from dissent.

CULTURAL DIVERSITY

The term *diversity* has become a part of the general social lexicon in recent years. We understand diversity to be variety and variation among people in a particular social space or larger society. **Cultural diversity** involves variation by physical appearance, material culture, and nonmaterial culture. It is important to go beyond physical appearance when examining diversity because, in reality, our differences extend to levels of education, the foods we like, whether we own or rent housing, and our beliefs and values. The material and nonmaterial resources that a person possesses contributes to their **cultural capital**, social assets that facilitate social mobility. The United States is one of the most culturally diverse places on Earth due its Indigenous, immigrant, and involuntarily relocated inhabitants. The 1970s television program *Schoolhouse Rock!* touted the United States as a cultural "melting pot," while critiques and progressives later advocated for the use of "salad bowl" instead. These contrasting views of the U.S. population remain in contemporary society in the form of political positions and initiatives that encourage a common culture, or a national identity, and those who support an inclusive culture that is tolerant of cultural variety.

Subcultures

Individuals and groups who do not see themselves (or are not accepted) as part of the dominant culture may find themselves to be a part of a **subculture**, or a segment of society with distinct cultural patterns. Subcultures can include "gamers," "Cub fans," or "Black Lives Matter activists." Most members of society participate in subcultures with higher or lower levels of commitment, so we should not think of subculture as inferior to dominant culture. However, the distinction is important because we must recognize that the dominant culture tends to align with the more powerful segments of a population. While we all reside under the umbrella of a dominant culture, cultural diversity inherently produces supplementary forms of culture and distinct cultural groups.

Countercultures

Cultural diversity includes not only conformity to conventional ideas or behaviors, but outright rejection as well. **Counterculture** refers to the challenge, contradiction, or rejection of dominant or mainstream culture. Modern countercultures can include groups referred to as "minimalists," those who choose lifestyles that leave a smaller ecological footprint by reducing consumerism, energy use, and so forth to the Older Order Amish who often live separate from the rest of a population, some refraining to even use power from electrical grids. Like subcultures, countercultures have a beneficial function in society as they reveal a social order that is often invisible and unquestioned. Countercultures only exist in response to a dominant culture that is believed to be inadequate or even harmful to some members of society. Countercultural ideas are flourishing in contemporary society due to increasing dissatisfaction with government and authoritative bodies. Mass media, particularly the internet, has allowed countercultural ideas to be transmitted in company with dominant cultural ideas. Subcultures and countercultures challenge **ethnocentrism**, the notion the dominant culture is a standard in which to judge others. Ethnocentric views about cultural difference distort not only perceptions of one's own culture, but that of others as well.

Applying Sociology: Taboo Tunes

Music, like sports and food, coalesces billions of people around the world. We now have access to genres of music from all over the world that can be played on radios, televisions, smartphones, and tablets. However, not all regions and governments are receptive of certain kinds of music. Throughout U.S. history, numerous songs and albums have been censored or banned. This music was thought to corrupt the minds of Americans, particularly youth, by encouraged drug use, promiscuous sex, and violence. The following timeline shows a condensed history of songs or albums that were banned or censored in the United States. As you review the timeline, reflect on the year of the song's release and corresponding social phenomena. Also take note of the genre of music in which the songs come from.

Taboo Songs Timeline

1939: Some U.S. cities banned "Strange Fruit" by Billie Holiday because of concern that it would provoke civil disharmony.

1944: "Rum and Coca-Cola" by the Andrews Sisters was banned because of lyrics describing getting drunk in a foreign country.

1946: "A-Huggin and A-Chalkin" by Johnny Mercer was banned from the BBC (British Broadcasting Radio) presumably because of its depiction of death.

1953: "Three Strands of Glass" by Webb Pierce was banned by some radio stations because it supposedly advocated drinking.

1954: "Honey Love" by the Drifters was banned by some radio stations due to "suggestive lyrics."

1960: "Will You Still Love Me Tomorrow" by The Shirelles was banned by radio stations for its mild sexual content.

1965: "I Can't Get No Satisfaction" by the Rolling Stones was banned by radio stations across the country due to sexually suggestive lyrics.

1968: "Unknown Soldier" by the Doors was banned from many radio stations because of its antiwar theme.

1975: "The Pill" by Loretta Lynn was banned by numerous country music stations because of the song talks about a woman taking birth control to prevent pregnancy.

1986: "Papa Don't Preach" by Madonna was not played on some radio stations because the song tells a story of teenage pregnancy.

1988: "F*ck the Police" by NWA was banned from stations not only because of the song's title, but because of its focus on police brutality and racial profiling.

1992: "Killing in the Name" by Rage Against the Machine was banned on radio due to its objection of police brutality and institutional racism.

2000: "Goodbye Earl" by the Dixie Chicks was refused radio play because of lyrics describing a victim of domestic abuse who poisons her husband.

2001: "Walk On" by U2 was banned in Myanmar because the song demonstrated support for the country's democratic movement and was dedicated to activist Daw Aung San Suu Kyi, who was placed under house arrest for her activism.

2003: "F*ck It (I Don't Want You Back)" by Eamon was banned from many United Kingdom radio stations because of its profanity.

2009: "LoveGame" by Lady Gaga was banned from radio due to what some considered highly suggestive themes.

2011: "Red Nation" by The Game was banned from BET, MTV, and numerous radio stations due to its references to gang life.

1. Recall an example from your own life in which a song, book, or element of material culture was banned or censored. What were the justifications given?
2. What does censoring an aspect of material culture, such as a song, say about the nonmaterial culture of an organization or society?
3. Discuss how censorship can serve to both maintain the status quo or a particular social order and cause opposition and rebellion.

CULTURAL TRANSMISSION

As previously stated, technological advancement has created opportunities for communication that are unprecedented. Societies around the world now have more contact and information about one another than ever before. There may not be a *global culture* so to speak, but global linkages have made the world's cultures much more similar. While English is the content language for over 60% of websites, only 25.9% of internet users use English, followed by Mandarin (19.4%) and Spanish (7.9%). These numbers show the increasing linguistic diversity of both internet content and internet users (Johnson, 2020; W3Techs, 2021).

Ways of Sharing
We will revisit technology and the mass media in a moment, but let's first explore cultural transmission on the micro level. Obviously, speech or spoken language has been the historical and traditional way in which information and ideas were exchanged and transmitted for centuries. We can refer to this as **cultural reproduction** or the transmission of cultural information, ideas, values, and beliefs throughout generations. Cultural reproduction can take the form of learning your great, great, great-grandfather's sourdough bread recipe or Muslims who memorize the entirety of the Qur'an and teach it orally and textually in Qur'anic schools and Islamic education institutions.

Ways of Adopting
In a globally connected and interdependent world there is a significant amount of cultural borrowing that takes place. In places like the United States, immigrants have brought with them distinct cultural foods, clothing, religions, and practices. Some of these things are adopted by the larger society and modified to cater to the dominant culture. For example, many Asian- or Latin American-inspired foods are slightly (or drastically) different in the United States than in the places in which they originated. A global economy allows people around the world to access clothing, accessories, and products made in other countries. Case in point are the numerous items sold in U.S. markets that are "made in China." Cultural diffusion, whether it is the transference of people or the transference of products, can

generate change in societies. Introducing something new can lead to subtle or more significant changes in the adopting society. For instance, while it is more affordable to employ Chinese workers to manufacture U.S. products, job outsourcing has led to the loss of many jobs for U.S. workers.

CULTURAL CHANGE

Culture is not static; it is subject to change as time progresses and societies evolve. Consider dominant cultural beliefs about interracial marriage prior to the *Loving v. Virginia* Supreme Court decision of 1967. Now, one in six newlyweds in the United States are married to someone of a different race or ethnicity (Brown & Livingston, 2017). The increasing pervasiveness of mass media has highlighted some of its shortcomings: bias media framing and imagery, a lack of inclusive, non-stereotypical representation, and problematic if not erroneous cultural narratives.

Multidisciplinary artist Alexandra Bell engages in work that identifies and challenges racial and gender biases embedded in news media. Bell explores how racism and sexism persist within cultural narratives. In 2018 she developed an art series entitled "Counternarratives" that calls attention to the biases and presumptions in popular news stories and then offers a reframing of those stories. In the 21st century, many independent media outlets have been developed by individuals and groups who seek to tell their own stories and shift dominant narratives. Sometimes culture is re-invented, and other times it comes back around like bell bottom jeans. Regardless of the direction it takes, change is inevitable.

SUMMARY: CONNECTING THE PIECES

Although identifying the intricacies of culture may take close examination and analysis, culture has been made visible in modern times due to its use to mainstream media. The persistent emphasis on cultural differences, namely race, class, gender, and immigrant status, has enlivened culture and made it subject to both praise and criticism. The dominant culture establishes a blueprint for society by constructing reality through ideologies, imagery, and behavioral standards. Our values, beliefs, and even our ethics and morals are guided by cultural standards.

Less influential cultures, like subcultures and countercultures, provide alternative ways of living and behaving and show dissent from what is normative. Cultural variation is important because it offers alternative and supplementary ways of thinking, living, and behaving. Culture has been described as the mortar that holds society together, but it may not be as fixed as a mortar. Culture is malleable, and we have seen just how fluid it can be with all the cultural changes that have taken place over time.

REVIEW AND CRITICAL THINKING

Directions: Respond to the questions and prompts, based on what you have learned in this chapter:

1. Describe two examples of nonmaterial culture and two examples of material culture.
2. Discuss how nonmaterial culture influences material culture, and vice versa.
3. Distinguish ethnocentrism and cultural relativism.
4. Describe how culture aids in the social construction of reality.
5. What factors have contributed to a global culture?
6. Discuss three ways cultural is transmitted.
7. In what ways does the mass media both perpetuate traditional cultural values and reveal alternative and supplementary cultural perspectives?

Credits
IMG 2.1: Sol Mednick, https://commons.wikimedia.org/wiki/File:Peter,_Paul_and_Mary_publicity_photo.jpg, 1970.
IMG 2.2: Daniel Zuchnik, https://www.teenvogue.com/gallery/tshirts-protest-slogans-donate-causes. Copyright © by Daniel Zuchnik/Getty Images.
IMG 2.3: Ohio Department of Transportation, https://commons.wikimedia.org/wiki/File:MUTCD-OH_D5-H20.svg, 2004.
IMG 2.4: Copyright © 2020 by Lorie Shaull (CC BY-SA 2.0) at https://commons.wikimedia.org/wiki/File:We_are_all_in_this_together_message_on_the_theatre_marquee_of_the_Paradise_Center_for_the_Arts_in_downtown_Faribault,_Minnesota_(49829800612).jpg.

■ CHAPTER 3

Socialization

Socialization can be defined as the lifelong process by which we learn what it means to be human in the world and in the cultural context of our society, begins at birth and continues until the end of life. Although infants do not immediately have a "sense of self," their awareness begins to develop upon their entrance into the world. Their biological senses acquaint them with smell, touch, and the feel of things and people around them. They hear sounds and language directed spe-

Image 3.1

cifically at them with the use of eye contact. Little humans continue to absorb essential lessons about human life and behavior from their home environments, until one day they reach an age at which they begin to spend time in daycare centers, preschools, and elementary schools. In these social settings, children began to develop more concrete ideas about their gender, ethnic, and even social class identities. The first peer groups form, which not only highlight common interests and orientations, but reveal individual idiosyncrasies. Elementary schools in particular develop practices that facilitate uniformity and homogenous behavior such as learning to stand in line, reciting a school pledge each day, or crossing legs during "rug time." These practices serve many functions but foremost allow teachers, staff, and administrators to carry out required academic tasks. In the featured photo (blurred for anonymity), is a second-grade class at Southside Elementary School. Students in the era of COVID-19 had to learn precautionary practices to protect their health and the health of others. The students pictured were taught to extend their arms to establish the desired distance needed between themselves and other students. The multicolor dots on the floor provide additional indications of where each student should stand. Within the school, classroom desks are socially distanced and face masks are required. Operating schools during the COVID-19 pandemic has necessitated a rethinking of spatial arrangements and the development of styles of teaching and learning. Students and educators alike are undergoing new forms of socialization that are unique to their social circumstances.

✓ CHAPTER OBJECTIVES

After completing this chapter students should be able to do the following:

✔ **Discuss** types of socialization and socialization processes throughout the life span.

✔ **Describe** the significance of socialization.

✔ **Explain** how deviance and conformity are learned.

✔ **Discuss** some of social-psychological the theories of human development.

✔ **Describe** primary agents of socialization and what they teach.

✔ **Identify** voluntary and involuntary resocialization experiences.

KEY TERMS

socialization	relativist determination	sensorimotor stage
nature	absolutist determination	preoperational stage
nurture	manifest function	formal operational stage
life chances	latent function	concrete operational stage
moral socialization	hidden curriculum	
deviant behavior	peer group	

THE SIGNIFICANCE OF SOCIALIZATION

Sociologist Kingsley Davis (1947) begins his essay "Extreme Isolation" with a discussion about what it means be human. He references an article he read that contained a section titled "Learning to be Human." Answering the questions of what it means to be human and how we learn to be human can give us insight into the role of socialization in human development. How different are we from animals? Are you really that different from your pet cat or dog? In most ways, as humans, we are indeed quite different. But what makes up these differences? Scientists and animal welfare advocates still have debates about whether animals have feelings or if they have more complex ways of communicating than we previously understood. However, this is not our task here. What we know for sure is that most humans *behave* quite differently than animals. In this chapter, we will explore what contributes to the development of specifically human behavior and how it varies across regions, groups, and identities.

The Effects of Isolation

Although we may not think much about these things as we age and progress through life, we were taught how to walk upright, feed ourselves with utensils, use the bathroom, and clean ourselves using products. Over time, we learned how to speak language(s), interact with others, and carry out particular roles. What would our lives and our relationships be like if we hadn't learned these things? Social scientists have examined case studies that provide insight into the impact of social isolation on human beings. In 1938, a Pennsylvania social worker discovered Anna, a 5-year-old child who had been kept in a second-floor storage room. When she was found, she was tied to a chair and extremely thin from malnourishment. From birth until nearly 6 years of age, Anna endured untreated medical conditions, lack of adequate nutrition, and very little attention and interaction with others. Anna was the child of a mentally impaired woman who was unmarried at the time of the birth. Anna was therefore considered "illegitimate," and her grandfather did not want such a child to stay in his home. When Anna was discovered, she had very little mental capacity: She could not speak, show expressions, and could barely walk.

After being removed from the home and placed into care centers where she received specialized treatment and training, Anna was able to name care workers, identify colors, walk and run, and eat regularly. Sadly, Anna lived only a year after making such significant strides in development. She succumbed to hemorrhagic jaundice in August of 1942 (Davis, 1947).

There are similar cases of isolated and institutionalized children: "Isabelle" (Davis, 1947), "The Wild Boy of Aveyron" (Lane, 1979), and "Genie" (Pines, 1981), to name a few. These cases illustrate that a lack of socialization can result in a range of mental and physical impairments and disabilities. Furthermore, interaction with other humans is what teaches us fundamental human traits and behaviors.

The Role of Nature and Nurture

Since the 20th century, "**nature**" or biological explanations of human behavior, has been heavily scrutinized. It is apparent that human beings are human beings anywhere in the world. Social scientists attribute our differences primarily to "**nurture**," the influences of our social environment and the cultural context in which we live. Human life and interaction centers around the functioning of the body. While humans share a similar physiology and body structure, the things that we eat, how often we exercise, and the likelihood of enduring bodily harm from accidents, are largely dependent on our social environment. The aforementioned and referenced cases of isolated and deprived children reveal the devasting effects of disruptions to human socialization. We can see similar patterns in animals that have been deprived of normal human interaction. Psychologists Harry and Margaret Harlow (1962) raised baby monkeys in isolation and found that they could not adjust to typical monkey life when placed with other monkeys. They did not know how to play, engage in pretend fights, or even have sexual intercourse.

In sum, we do not naturally develop into social adults. Socialization is what makes us human beings capable of achieving intellectual altitudes and carry out complex social roles. There are physical, mental, and social consequences to a lack of socialization. While one may be able to overcome them, developmental incompetency impacts one's life trajectory, or what sociologists call **life chances**, the probability that a person's life will follow a certain path and turn out a certain way. Therefore, society "makes us human" because it is through human contact that people learn to be members of the human community.

Applying Sociology: Nature and Nurture

Read the examples of characteristics and determine whether they are influenced by nature, nurture, or both. Circle your selection. Provide a rationale for each decision.

Appetite: Nature | Nurture | Both
Rationale:

_____

_____

Athletic ability: Nature | Nurture | Both
Rationale:

_____

_____

Personality: Nature | Nurture | Both
Rationale:

Friendliness: Nature | Nurture | Both
Rationale:

CONSTRUCTING DEVIANCE
Deviance lies in the eye of the beholder.

Relativist Determinations of Deviance

One of the key *types* of socialization that humans undergo is **moral socialization**. Moral socialization is the teaching and learning of specific messages and practices concerning what is right and wrong, good and bad, desirable and undesirable. Socialization, along with our experiences in life, provide us with ideas about deviance that relate to morality, safety, and how deviant behavior should be dealt with. If we define **deviant behavior** as actions or ways of being that do not conform to the norms or values of a society or culture, then most people would be considered deviants. In fact, most people are deviants. Most people do or say things that run contrary to social norms, expectations, or ideals. Have you ever lied? Have you ever driven over the speed limit? When was the last time that you cursed? Each of these behaviors are socially deviant. However, deviance is *relative*. This means that deviance is not inherent in any particular act, condition, or belief. Instead, it is socially constructed, a culmination of human judgements and ideas. A **relativist determination** of deviance would account for the fact that there is cultural variation in what is recognized as deviance, as well as if and how deviant actions are penalized. For example, wearing dreadlocks as a hairstyle is commonplace among Rastafarians in Jamaica and Ethiopia, but the hairstyle has been intermittently banned in many cities and states across the United States. Like wearing hooded sweatshirts, in many schools dreadlocks are often viewed as "inappropriate" or violations to school dress codes (Belsha, 2020).

Absolutist Determinations of Deviance

Discretionary bans and penalties for certain hairstyles align with an **absolutist determination** of deviance. Absolutist determinations of deviance uphold a binary framework that categorizes behavior as good and proper or bad and improper. Absolutist conceptions of deviance suggest something about society's relationship with the person or behavior considered deviant. A deviant is therefore considered different from ordinary members of society and deserves to be treated differently. Absolutist conceptions of deviance often employ stereotypes and are oversimplified. More often that not, racial and cultural minority populations are more heavily impacted by these conceptions (Newman, 2012). Due to the influences of nature and nurture, as human beings we thrive from a sense of belonging. It does not feel good to be left out or "othered," and most people work very hard to avoid this sort of isolation. However, this kind of social isolation is not always avoidable if a person embodies a skin color or hair texture that has been deemed inherently deviant. Therefore, moral socialization functions to construct images and perceptions of people that transcend their actual behaviors. Preconceived notions and dominant ideologies are used to form impressions of people that we do not even know, presuming their social value and contribution, or even their inclination to "good" or "bad" behaviors.

AGENTS OF SOCIALIZATION

We can now acknowledge that socialization does not happen without the contributions of people and social experiences. The significant people, groups, and entities that shape our individual and social identities are called **agents of socialization**. Throughout the life span, agents of socialization change and have varying impact. Agents of socialization have primary and secondary influences depending on the length and frequency of exposure and their context and familiarity. Examples of agents of socialization include family, peers, neighborhoods, religion, school, and mass media. We will examine a few of these agents in more detail and consider the specific types of socialization that they may provide.

Family

The first individuals that people typically have contact with are their families. These individuals may not be biological relatives since definitions of family are wide-ranging. A family can be the people that a person lives with or is cared for by, especially during their dependent years. It is within this context that we establish our initial beliefs, values, and ideas about who we are and what we want out of life. Family is a primary agent of socialization because our relationships with these individuals tend to be deep and long lasting.

Social class socialization

Children are not only inheritors of some of their family's physical characteristics, but recipients of their social class standing as well. A family's social class can make a difference in how children are socialized. Economic standing influences the resources that a family has, such as toys, books, and technology. The nature of a parent's work, their level of autonomy at work, and their ability to shape their work schedule can impact their model of childrearing. However, childrearing is multifaceted. While social class is influential, it is not determinant of how family's rear children or economic positions of children in later life (Lareau & Weininger, 2009).

Racial Socialization

An area in which parents contribute to a child's social identity is their race. Since race is a social construct (discussed more in upcoming chapters), societies define racial categories and the implications of racial characteristics. Like social class, racial groups are also stratified or placed within a hierarchy denoting their level of power, resources, and social value. Children learn at a very young age that their skin colors have meaning beyond merely colors. They begin to take note of how people of different skin colors are viewed and treated differently. Initially, these distinctions are perceived as natural. But as one progresses through life and becomes more conscious and educated, the influence of social systems and social arrangements in regulating life circumstances and outcomes for individuals and groups becomes more apparent.

School

As mentioned in the opening vignette, schools serve as important agents of socialization, not only for children, but young adults as well. Second perhaps to home life, schools are the primary sites where children learn and master social rules and regulations. In the home children learn guidelines and receive knowledge, but schools impart a broader perspective of the world and one's place within it. Schools carry out various **manifest functions**, or intended and expected functions, such as providing a formal education in subjects such as reading, writing, mathematics, history, and science. Additional subjects offered, how much time is spent on each subject, and resources supplied vary by school type and level of funding. Schools also have social dynamics that may not be a part of a standard curriculum or formal school practices or policies. These are the **latent functions** of schooling, or the unintended or unexpected consequences of the social system. For example, within school youth learn many cultural ideas about gender, sexuality, social class, and ethnicity. Sociologists refer to this phenomenon as the **hidden curriculum**, values and ideas that may not be explicitly taught but are conveyed in the subtext of class lessons, extracurricular activities, and conversations among classmates.

Peer Socialization

A **peer group** is a social group in which a person typically shares age, interests, and social position. Once a child enters an educational system, particularly public education, the peer group becomes a significant agent of socialization. A peer group allows youth to form relationships outside of direct adult supervision. Peer groups become very influential is shaping attitudes about culture and behavior. Furthermore, peers often function as role models, in which young people may copy one another's clothing styles, slang, and future aspirations.

Gender Socialization

Schools, in combination with family, socialize youth into gender roles. While families do the initial work of naming, clothing, and treating children among gender lines, schools reinforce dominant ideologies about gender. In her paper examining gender socialization cross-nationally, Nelly P. Stromquist (2007), concluded that schools engage in substantial gender ideology formation and transmission through classroom practices, teachers' attitudes and expectations, and peer socialization. She found the following:

- Much of the gender construction in schools creates very distinct notions of what it means to be a man and a woman, with polarized attributes for femininity and masculinity. This construction is similar across levels of education and intensifies as the time in school expands.
- Across most countries, boys continue to dominate classroom time and space, a practice that seems to create subdued girls and naturalizes differences between men and women.
- Academic performance of boys and girls is moving toward convergence, but notions remain about fields of study and occupations that result in clustering by gender.
- The curriculum, especially sex education, continues to center on biological features and refuses to acknowledge social dimensions of adolescent sexuality and treats sex as an issue to be controlled by others.
- Peers contribute powerfully to the climate of classrooms and to the re-enactment of conventional sexual norms. In the peer culture, boys feel pressured to be less academically oriented.
- While many teachers are women, their own lack of professional training on gender issues does not build on their potential as role models for transformative work or as advocates for gender social justice.
- Most public education policies fail to recognize the socialization role of schools and to address detrimental effects through intensive counter measures. Overall, little progress can be detected in the past decade in terms of transformations in policy and practice from a gender perspective.

Mass Media

Mass media builds reality as we internalize its messages.

Consumption

In the 21st century, the mass media has emerged as a social instituticn. The expansion, capacity, use, and influence of social media has made it a key agent of socialization. An impersonal mode of communication and information transmission has shaped the personal lives of millions of people. The Nielson (2018) Total Audience Report, a culmination of research that gathers data on what Americans read, watch, and listen to, revealed that U.S. adults (18-plus years) spend nearly half a day interacting with media. Julia Jacobo of ABC News reported that in 2019 teens spent more than 7 hours a day on screens for entertainment. The American Academy of Child and Adolescent Psychiatry reported in 2020 that, on average, children ages 8–12 in the United States spend 4–6 hours a day watching or using screens. Often before children learn to read, they watch television, movies, and play video games.

Impact

Computers, e-books, and web-based programs have become commonplace in American schools. Time spent using media often results in less time spent in face-to-face interactions and forming meaningful bonds. While mass media has contributed many positive and progressive aspects to human life, it also has negative behavioral consequences. Too much mass media consumption, particularly on screens, can contribute to sleep problems, lower grades in school, and the development of poor self-image. These things are dependent on various factors such as the length of time viewing, types of media, and times of day in which it is used.

Applying Sociology: Types of Socialization

Fill in the chart with three types of socialization that you have experienced, the agent of socialization, the social setting, and the lesson learned. Respond to the questions that follow.

Type of Socialization	Agent of Socialization	Location or Social Setting	Lesson/Influence

1. Discuss how both the agent of socialization and the social setting shape how one interprets and receives socializing messages.
2. Have any of the lessons learned from socialization been revised or omitted as you have gotten older and had various experiences in the world? Explain.

THEORIES OF HUMAN DEVELOPMENT

Many researchers across varying disciplines have contributed to our understanding of human development. Therefore, debate exists about the processes through which "the self" emerges and develops. The following discussion will highlight a couple of researchers who have studied human development from psychological and sociological orientations.

George Herbert Mead and the Development of the Social Self

As referenced in Chapter 1, George Herbert Mead (1863–1931) contributed ideas that have been formational in the theoretical framework of symbolic interaction. Symbolic interactionists emphasize the role of symbols and socially constructed meaning in shaping social interaction. Mead's work sought to explain how social experience helps to develop individual personality and the emergence of **the self**, the part of an individual's personality composed of self-awareness and self-image. According to Mead, infants and very young children develop into social beings by mimicking the actions of those around them. This happens most often in the context of play. During play, children develop an understanding of themselves as "me" and "I," with "I" being spontaneous and consumed with wants and desires and "me" being the social self, with the ability to see themselves through the eyes of others (Giddens et. al., 2017). Mead posited that in later stages of child development, children take part is organized games in which they learn rules and notions of fairness, intention, and shared participation.

Jean Piaget and Cognitive Development Theory

Swiss theorist Jean Piaget (1896–1980) described cognitive development through distinct stages in which humans interpret what they see, hear, and feel in the world around them. In the first stage of development, called the **sensorimotor stage**, individuals experience the world only through their senses. This stage ranges from birth to about age 2. You can observe children of this age frequently putting things into their mouths and touching objects around them. They learn that their environment has unique and stable features and begin to understand the difference between people and objects.

In the second stage, called the **preoperational stage**, humans begin to think about the world mentally, establishing meaning through symbols and language. This stage can last from age 2 to about 7 years. In this stage, individuals tend to interpret the world from their own position. They can identify a toy as their "favorite" but cannot explain what kinds of toys they like.

Next comes the **concrete operational stage**, occurring from age 7 to approximately 11 years. In this stage, individual thinking is based primarily on physical perceptions of the world. Causal connections in one's surroundings are made, and logic is used to understand how and why things happen. At this stage a person can use multiple symbols at a time. For instance, they can understand that a particular day is "Wednesday" and their birthday.

The last stage identified by Piaget is the **formal operational stage**. At this stage of development, individuals can think abstractly and critically. This stage can range from age 12 through young adulthood. When faced with a problem, a person in this stage will consider multiple ways to solve problems and think through each scenario critically. This stage of human development is not universal and can be influenced by one's education and knowledge received from their social environment.

Piaget watched his own three children grow and evolve as he developed this theory. We can witness the use of Piaget's stages of development in modern daycare centers in which rooms, its components, and the curriculum are specific to age and various stages of development.

RESOCIALIZATION

As we progress through life, we take on a variety of statuses, roles, and identities. When we learn new norms, values, attitudes, and behaviors to match a new situation; this is called **resocialization**. Resocialization experiences can be, but not always, quite different from previous experiences in life. Prior life experiences can also inform resocialization experiences. Some experiences can be subtle and mild, like training for a new job, or sudden with intense impact, such as being imprisoned for a crime. The experience of resocialization is largely shaped by whether the change is voluntary or involuntary.

Voluntary

Voluntary resocialization means exactly that, voluntarily taking on a new role that accompanies behavioral changes. For example, when a person becomes a student, they voluntarily choose to have a resocialization experience. Unlike involuntary resocialization, these experiences are wide ranging, from the student who joins the basketball team to the formerly incarcerated individual who later becomes a community mentor.

Involuntary

Imposed or involuntary resocialization is usually more immediately impactful than voluntary resocialization. Consider the experiences of imprisonment, mental health institutionalization, and mandatory boot camps. These entities are referred to by Erving Goffman (1961) as **total institutions**, places where people are cut off from the rest of society and where they come under nearly the complete control of officials in charge. Total institutions are usually isolated from the public, and gates, guards, and checkpoints serve to regulate outside contact. Total institutions undoubtedly leave a lasting impact on individuals, even after their exit.

SUMMARY: CONNECTING THE PIECES

Socialization is a complex, lifelong process. We develop human potential and social awareness through the socialization process. Without proper socialization, significant mental and behavior impairments can ensue. Through various agents of socialization, we are shown and taught familial and social values and expectations, which gear us for involvement in the social system.

Through social interaction we establish a sense of self and knowledge of our surroundings. Throughout the life course we make transitions, voluntarily or involuntarily, by taking on new statuses and roles. Although socialization has a powerful impact on our lives, we are human with freewill. Therefore, individual behavior is hard to predict. We are all actively involved in the construction of self and our social reality. The self, in concert with the options available within our environments and societies, shape our development and behavior.

REVIEW AND CRITICAL THINKING

Directions: Respond to the questions and prompts, based on what you have learned in this chapter:

1. Discuss the ways socialization contributes to mental and social development.
2. Describe the role that "nurture" plays in the manifestation and expression of heredity ("nature") characteristics.
3. How are ideas about deviance taught through the socialization process?
4. What are agents of socialization? What types of socialization do they provide?
5. Describe one of the theories of human development.
6. How does resocialization differ from socialization?
7. Discuss an example of voluntary and involuntary resocialization.

■ CHAPTER 4

Social Structure

W ork sucks. This is a phrase uttered by some or all employees at one time or another. But what is it that makes work *suck*? Work provides our income and ability to sustain our daily lives. It allows individuals to contribute their various skills, talents, and knowledge. It is a social space conducive to forming friendships or even romantic partnerships. Work provides structure to our lives.

Image 4.1

Ironically, these are the same things that can make work suck sometimes. Employment resides within a social structure created for efficiency and production. Therefore, one's feelings, emotions, or personal life are often less significant than the functioning of the system. **Social structure** can be defined as a largely invisible system that broadly shapes and constrains human activity in noticeable and predictable ways. Although the movie *Office Space* may exaggerate the mundanity of office work, it depicts very accurately the ways in which the procedural mandates of modern employment are often sacrificial to worker autonomy. Additionally, work does not always provide enough income for the countless bills and expenses of residents of highly industrialized countries. In many workplaces, mechanization and technological equipment has reduced the need for individual input and creativity. Advances in artificial intelligence have shown, quite literally, the robotic nature of modern work by using robots as workers! The gains of industrial and technological advancement often come with the loss of some things that are inherently human. This chapter will further detail the balance of human and nonhuman aspects of social structure that interplay and influence one another.

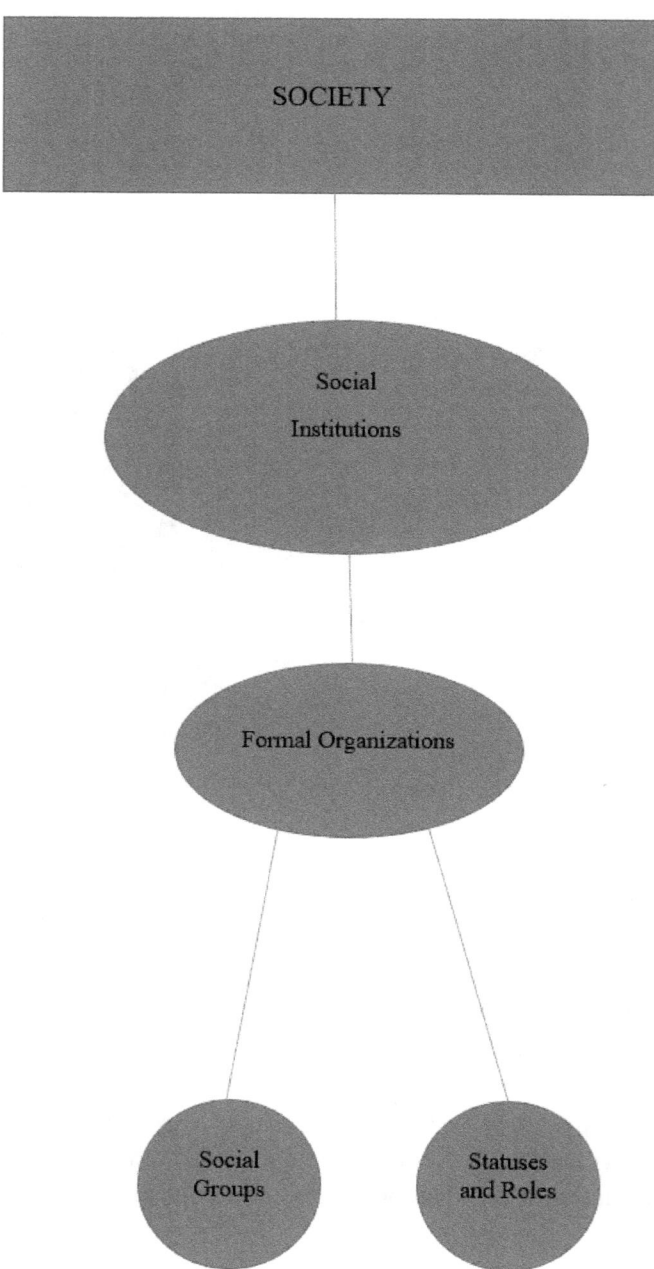

Image 4.2

✔ CHAPTER OBJECTIVES

After completing this chapter students should be able to do the following:

✔ **Discuss** each component of social structure and its elements.

✔ **Describe** employment at macro, meso, and micro levels of analyses.

✔ **Explain** the functions and problems of bureaucracy.

✔ **Discuss** the principles of McDonaldization by using a real-world example.

✔ **Define** *social interaction* and describe its connection to the symbolic interaction perspective.

✔ **Explain** different types of communication and their contribution to the social structure of a society.

KEY TERMS

Social structure

Social institutions

Emergent institutions

Bureaucracy

Rationalization

Impression management

Dramaturgical theory

Meta social structure

COMPONENTS OF SOCIAL STRUCTURE

The social structure of a society is largely invisible yet broadly shapes and constrains human activity in noticeable and predictable ways. One of the outcomes of a sociological under-standing is that we will ideally be able to perceive society as a system with various parts. When we think about local elections, we know that they are not isolated events in local communities but are linked to the operations of a larger political and governmental insti-tution. The social structure is comprised of foundational pillars like social institutions and formal organizations, with the contributions of various social groups. Figure 4.1 illustrates components of the social structure and their arrangement by level of society. As explained in Chapter 1, levels of society are macro, meso, and micro. Each level of analysis contains different components and offer unique analytical lenses.

Social Institutions

At the broader, macro-level of society are **social institutions**, organized sets of structures established to meet the fundamental survival needs of society and provide guidelines for behavior. Traditional social institutions include education, religion, and family. **Emergent social institutions**, or institutions that have come to be over time with the advancement of science, technology, and geopolitics include mass media, military, and sports. Each of these institutions has hierarchies of power and decision-making. They are comprised of various formal organizations and social groups that support and carry out the mission of the institution. Due to the interconnection and interdependency or all parts of the social system, failures and shortcomings of any social institution impact the entirety of the social structure. Some institutions have more power and influence than others. For instance, in the United States a democratic political system and a capitalism economic system significantly shape the operations of other institutions and organizations.

Formal Organizations

Formality in modern organizations is often a requirement for legal standing. In order to obtain legal accreditation, colleges and universities must meet specific written standards regarding things like grading policies and faculty adherence to antidiscrimination policies, such as Title IX. In a historical period in which about 8 billion people are geographically dispersed around the world, yet interconnected through personal relationships, work, and the supply and demand of resources, a substantial amount of coordination is needed. **Formal organizations**, which are organizations that are rationally designed to meet certain objectives by means of using explicit rules, regulations, and procedures, provide a framework for coordinating activities and resources. Sociologist Max Weber (1978) emphasized that the development of organizations depends on the control of information. Weber viewed organizations as hierarchical, with power typically concentrated at the top. Organizations have the ability to both connect and clash with the principles of democracy that lean toward broad representation and the ability of citizens to influence and shape social life.

Social Groups

Social groups, or collections of people who share a common identity and regularly interact with one another, are innumerable throughout society. They range from large, impersonal groups, called **secondary groups**, to small, more intimate groups, referred to as **primary groups**. Our earliest socialization experiences likely occurred with primary groups such as our family and friends. These groups are characterized by face-to-face interaction and a strong sense of commitment. By contrast, secondary group relationships are often fleeting and impersonal. Examples of secondary groups include schools, work groups, and athletic clubs. There are seldom emotional ties or long-lasting commitments in secondary groups. Almost all of our important social interactions take place within some type of social group. Social groups illustrate historical change as the types of groups and the nature of their relationships become more or less important as society evolves economically, politically, and socially. For instance, for most of human history interactions took place within primary groups. Nowadays, most of our social groups are likely secondary, concerned with accomplishing certain tasks.

Statuses and Roles

Ultimately, it is individuals who work in collaboration with others to maintain the various components of the social structure. Individuals take on **statuses**, or a person's rank or position in a particular context, to carry out a variety of **roles**, the expected behaviors of a person who occupies a particular status. A status can be *ascribed*, bestowed upon birth, *achieved*, acquired through personal effort, ability, or choice, or *master*, overshadowing all other statuses that a person occupies. Ascribed statuses include variables such as age or sex assignment. A student or a teacher would be considered achieved statuses. The master status determination is less clear as both the perceptions of others and personal perceptions shape what a person may consider a master status. For instance, being a categorically Latinx person may be viewed as a master status in larger society, while individual Latinx people may consider their gender or immigrant status as more significant in shaping their personal identity.

BUREAUCRACY AND MCDONALDIZATION

The film *Office Space* illustrates bureaucracy in a comedic, though cynical light. While bureaucracy provides structure and organization to social life, it often supersedes human ingenuity and prospects for change. In sociology, **bureaucracy** is a larger hierarchical organization that is governed by formal rules and regulations and has a clear specification of tasks. Bureaucracy is most noticeable in the areas of work, production, and consumption, but is present in nearly all areas of social and personal life. Weber's (1992) conception of **rationalization** undergirds bureaucracy, the process whereby action based on tradition or emotion is replaced by instrumental rational action. Using the "means to an end" analogy, in the operation of bureaucracy, the "end" becomes more significant than the "means." The "means" has significance only in its contribution to the "end." In this framework, human feelings, emotions, and personal contributions are second tier to the goals of the organization or institution.

Features of Bureaucracy

The primary features of bureaucratic organization include the following:

- a division of labor
- a hierarchy of authority
- an impersonal environment
- formal rules and regulations
- standard operating procedures

If we use the example of a college, we can see the *division of labor* among administrators, staff, faculty, and students. The division of labor also reflects a *hierarchy of authority*, in which groups or individuals at the top of the division of labor also tend to have the most power and authority in the institution. An *impersonal environment* is constructed in colleges, like many other areas of social life, through the use of email and mailed correspondence as the primary mode of communication. Aside from classes and activities that take place in-person on campus, students may never know the administrators, staff, faculty, or larger student body of the college. In the increasingly virtual nature of communication, numerous students never step foot on college campuses and instead exclusively enroll in online courses.

Documents like employee contracts, collective bargaining agreements, and student codes of conduct make the *formal rules and regulations* of a college very clear. These documents are binding agreements regarding the expectations and prohibitions of behavior on campus. They have both social and legal ramifications. Formal rules and regulations shape the *standard operating procedures* of an institution. Every area of the social structure carries out various routine operations, and colleges are no exception. Faculty must prepare and show up to teach their classes, deans manage the operation of various academic departments, secretaries facilitate intercollegiate communications and oversee office business, custodians and technicians ensure that the facilities are functional and clean, and the list goes on. Each group is given particular responsibilities in the operation of the college campus that are explicitly expressed and uniformly carried forward.

On the Clock

Since the establishment of World Standard time in 1884, humans have been captivated by the concept of time. Prior to 1884, time was not clear or definite. Many Indigenous tribes used star patterns in the night sky to determine seasons and travel. In the eyes of the Ojibwe people, one of the largest groups of Native Americans on the North American continent, the constellation Orion was and still is referred to as the Wintermaker (King, 2014). For centuries, the five daily Islamic prayers have been determined by the position of the sun in the sky. In some societies, time was measured with tools like pendulums or the migration of animals. These things provided general and rough estimates of time, which were fine for early societies in which daily life was not structured around a 24-hour clock.

As the global population increased, particularly in Western societies, and international trade and relations became commonplace, more precise scheduling aided in the integration of people and resources into time and space. The clock is a necessary component for capitalist economies with workers who check in and out based on schedules. Punctuality is a cultural ideal and a behavioral expectation. In the United States tardiness is viewed as disrespectful or even sinful in some contexts. The confines of time can be particularly challenging for individuals who must accomplish certain tasks within a fixed timeframe. In July of 2017, during a House Financial Services Committee hearing, Congress member Maxine Waters asked Treasury Secretary Steven Mnuchin why he hadn't responded to a letter she'd sent him in May requesting information about former president Donald Trump's financial ties. When Mnuchin averted the question, Waters chastised him for wasting her allotted time and urged him to answer the question. When he continued to forestall the question, Waters responded, "Reclaiming my time." She repeated the phrase again and again until the committee chairman silenced Mnuchin. The phrase has since become a media sensation, used in numerous memes and cited in popular music (Greene, 2017; Williams, 2017).

Expanded information technologies like smartphones and social media have created a pathway for our work life to spill into our leisure time as well. YouTube commentator Saint Andrewism, in his video "The Tyranny of the Clock," encourages us to again use clocks as a tool of reference and coordination and not as a dominating force in our lives. He states how difficult it is to focus on the present while beholden to a ticking clock. Our present states are often neglected due to concern about upcoming responsibilities and what the future may hold. However, he says, unlike the past or the future, the present is the only thing that we know we have.

McDonaldization

The term **McDonaldization**, coined by George Ritzer in his 1993 book *The McDonaldization of Society*, refers to the increasing presence of the fast-food business model in common social institutions. McDonaldization goes beyond the workings of one of the most prolific fast-food restaurants in the world. Additionally, the concept uncovers the interests imbedded in social design and arrangement. Through the lens of McDonaldization we can view the interplay of multiple institutions at various levels.

Principles of McDonaldization are (a) efficiency, (b) calculability, (c) predictability, and (d) control. **Efficiency** involves methods to ensure that desired ends are met in the shortest amount of time possible. In the context of fast-food restaurants like McDonald's a drive-through option embodies the concept of efficiency. Although drive-through and self-service options require more effort and labor from consumers, these options are popular and accepted because they hasten the speed of transactions. **Calculability** refers to numerical indicators of both the result and speed of a product or service. For example, you can expect to wait 30 minutes for an oil change at Pennzoil or diet pills that guarantee weight loss within a specific span of days. Many individuals who choose a drive-through option do so because they find it faster and more convenient. They do not expect to wait in line for an hour. Calculability is also related to quantity, whereas more food for less money is seen as "a good deal."

The principle of **predictability** is the expectation that a product or service will be consistent regardless of the place it is offered or at what time. To achieve this goal, companies may use specific types of produce (like McDonalds's Russet potatoes used for French fries) or products that are genetically modified to facilitate uniformity. Beyond restaurants, we can also predict what to expect when we shop at a retail store or visit a dentist. While each visit may not be *exactly* the same, they usually do not veer far from our assumptions. **Control** as a principle of McDonaldization involves the use of technology and digital tools that ensure accuracy and objectivity. Since humans are fluid beings with varying and uncertain emotions, attention, and personal experiences, "smart" technology resources serve to control interactions while at the same time reduce the labor needed by employees.

While bureaucracy and the principles of McDonaldization are extremely beneficial to those who benefit from the heightened levels of production that stem from the social structure, these methods can create dehumanizing practices that lower the value of human contribution and well-being. The endeavor to provide services and products in this fashion often produces irrationalities in supposedly rational systems (Weber 1992).

SOCIAL INTERACTION

Social interaction within the social structure is largely shaped by the social setting in which it occurs. Each social setting is a governing structure with its own guidelines and expectations for behavior. The socialization process teaches us to adapt to the expectations of different realms of the social arena. For instance, we likely dress, act, and may even talk differently in a school setting than we would if we were at a friend's home. Both the social setting and *who we are* in that particular setting influence how we interact with one another. Social interaction is an interplay of people, things, ideas, and constraints. It is a fundamental aspect of the social structure and the foundation upon which social order relies. Social interaction includes not only an array of behavioral processes but mechanisms for the recovery of failed or "spoiled" interactions.

Impression Management

One does not need to take a sociology class to learn that people care about how they are perceived by others. We engage in **impression management** to present ourselves to others in ways that will lead them to view us in a favorable light. Sociologist Erving Goffman (1922–1982) used the analogy of a theatrical performance, or the **dramaturgical theory**, to explain social interaction in everyday life. According to Goffman (1959), social life can be depicted as a stage on which people interact. Depending on the occasion, we are either actors or members of "the audience." Throughout our daily activities we carry out various roles or "parts," and these ongoing performances shape who we are. Therefore, the self is not static, but constructed and reconstructed from social situations in which people attempt to create specific impressions in the minds of others. Impressions are privately managed "backstage" before we appear in the "frontstage." For example, most people will clean themselves, style their hair, and put on nice clothes *before* their date arrives (backstage) to take them to dinner. Once the date arrives, individuals want to be prepared for the encounter and ensuing activities (frontstage).

Performances

Continuing with the dramaturgical theory, behavior is changed in accordance to changes in the nature of the audience. Since our lives in contemporary society are highly bureaucratized, it is easy to arrange what Goffman refers to as *audience segregation*, in which impressions are constructed for specific interactions with a particular audience. Through the use of audience segregation, we are able to show different faces to different people. This can sometimes be challenging in face-to-face interactions in which audiences may overlap, such as personal friends who are also coworkers or classmates. However, the internet and social media are uniquely constructed to facilitate audience segregation. People are able to maintain a variety of profiles and pages curated to portray ideal impressions for target audiences. Nevertheless, blurring audiences can still occur online and lead to personal catastrophes ranging from embarrassment to punitive measures taken by an employer.

META SOCIAL STRUCTURE: THE VIRTUAL SOCIAL STRUCTURE

Most of us could not have imagined the social impact of virtual platforms and interactions when the internet was invented in the later part of the 20th century. Today, the virtual world provides both a meta social structure and multidimensionality to our interactions. The **meta social structure** can be defined as a virtual social structure that runs parallel to physical structures. It is shaped by culture and shapes culture. It has components of materiality, but it is not always tangible or obvious (especially in its power). It not only includes virtual social spaces, but omnipresent technologies such as cameras, surveillance equipment, and digital tracking. An analysis of the meta social structure is an important part of media literacy because it is an arena of high social engagement and interaction that is increasingly being dominated and weaponized by the power structure. Media literacy not only involves the ability to recognize different types of media and their functions, but also to comprehend their mechanisms and ascertain their role across different contexts. In Sociology we recognize the media as an emergent social institution, but more than that, as a domain of power. It not only transmits information, but also creates ideology. It tells us what we should be thinking about and how we should be thinking about it. Therefore, it is coercive.

The meta social structure can be partnered with Karl Marx's concepts of base and superstructure. Marx wrote in the Preface to "A Contribution to the Critique of Political Economy" (1859), that 'the economic structure of society' forms the 'real basis' on which 'rises a legal and political superstructure.' Marx defined the base as the economic foundations of society (means of production) and the superstructure as the cultural, legal, and political systems. The meta social structure contains dimensions of the base and superstructure. However, it has its own economic foundations and transactions, a unique culture, the ability to shape narratives and ideologies, and to validate and sanction.

Through social media we can form online identities that may or may not align with who we really are. Impression management takes on a new dimension as we are able to carefully and strategically portray images of ourselves to the outside world. Unlike in real life, these impressions can be edited and transformed with relative ease. Through the "audience segregation" that multiple virtual platforms bestow, we are able to construct specific messaging and images such as "the respectable student" or "the professional"

(Giddens et. al, 2017). The potential for role conflict and role strain are apparent online as others can observe our images and actions and compare them to their own understanding about us.

The term *status* takes on a new meaning in virtual spaces, sometimes implying a person's current activity, and other times indicating one's involvement in an intimate relationship. The *roles* carried out in the virtual world are highly dependent upon the particular platform one is using. We know that on Instagram we are expected to post pictures and on Twitter we are to send quick and concise messages. The meta social structure, like physical social structures, governs the activity of participants through rules and guidelines for engagement. Those who deviate from prescribed behavioral or content expectations are subject to online suspensions, demonetization, or complete removal from a platforms (Guynn, 2019).

The meta social structure holds the same biases and prejudices as the physical social structure, and in some ways these problems are magnified due to the distance and shielding that online environments provide. For example, people are more likely to bully others and display bigotry online than they are in person. According to a 2016 Norton Cyber Security Insights Report, "48 percent of parents believe their children are more likely to be bullied online than on a playground" (para. 5). Many people succumb to the stress and pressures of the virtual world in which we are always "on" and inundated with the lives of others.

The virtual world even overlaps with the real world in economic forms, and not just for the creators of the multi-million and billion dollar platforms. Every day people can buy, sell, and trade online with virtual currencies such as Bitcoin and Ethereum. These crypto-currencies are widely accepted in exchange for real goods and services. Two online games, *Second Life* and *Entropia Universe*, allow players a two-way conversion of currencies; players can not only convert real money into in-game virtual currency, but they can also convert it back to real money (Chung, 2021).

The meta social structure of the virtual world is one to be considered and taken seriously as we examine social structure. Virtual reality has increasingly become a part of our physical and lived reality, bringing with it unique implications for society. This is an area for further sociological inquiry and research as we can expect its further development and influence on the lives of humans in years to come.

SEEING SOCIOLOGY: SOCIAL LIFE IN FILM

This chapter began by illustrating bureaucracy in the context of work as displayed in the movie *Office Space*. Films are reflections of the social and cultural aspects of a society and can help us to better understand the one in which we live. For years, students in my Introduction to Sociology class wrote a three-part course paper in which they sociologically analyzed a film. Films were analyzed using four interrelated themes: identity, interaction, inequality, and institutions. Students used the theme of identity to explore the development and transformation of characters throughout the film. They discussed the ways character identity and status played an important role in shaping interactions in the film. Students then wrote about one or more of the most significant social interactions in the film, focusing on communication patterns, the construction of meaning, character statuses and roles, and the social setting. The next theme for analysis was social institutions. Students were asked to identify the institutions that shaped the lives of the film's characters. The institutional analysis additionally revealed the social structure present or sometimes invisibly operating to shape identities and interactions of the cast. The last theme for examination was inequality. Students were encouraged to think about inequality beyond the film and make connections to similar inequalities in the real world. This practice aimed to illustrate how films are reflections of reality, and that some of the most brutal and unimaginable injustices depicted in cinema authentically impact the lives of people in the real world (Feltey & Sutherland, 2013).

Applying Sociology: Film Through Multiple Sociological Lenses

Using each of the major sociological theories, functionalism, conflict theory, symbolic interactionism, or the feminist theory, provide an analysis (or critique) of the Hollywood film industry.

1. Is one of the theories more useful than the others in analyzing the film industry?
2. If you were to carry out a study of the Hollywood film industry, which area would you focus your analysis?
3. What research method(s) would you use?

SUMMARY: CONNECTING THE PIECES

An understanding of social structure is integral to employing the sociological perspective. In our exploration of society as a social system, components of the social structure are the pillars that provide its foundation. This foundation is the basis on which social interaction takes place. Through social interaction, statuses and roles are executed which maintain social equilibrium. Our identities are actualized through contributions to the social structure at various levels. High levels of bureaucracy assist in the maintenance of predictable and consistent social operations that are advantageous to production but often unfavorable to human autonomy and expression. As a result of technological development, society has birthed another layer of social structure—a meta social structure in which both commerce and general social interactions take place virtually. This has added a new complexity to the social structure as we navigate and reconcile these simultaneous realities.

REVIEW AND CRITICAL THINKING

Directions: Respond to the questions and prompts, based on what you have learned in this chapter:

1. Discuss the key components of social structure and the level of society in which they can be found.
2. Distinguish between bureaucracy and McDonaldization.
3. Discuss the personal and social benefits and disadvantages of bureaucracy.
4. Discuss factors that shape social interaction, such as social setting, status, and norms.
5. Define impression management and provide an example of its use in daily life.
6. Describe the meta social structure and how it differs from the larger social structure.
7. What unique opportunities and challenges are produced as a result of the meta social structure.

Credit
IMG 4.1: Copyright © by LaurMG (CC BY-SA 3.0) at https://commons.wikimedia.org/wiki/File:Frustrated_man_at_a_desk_(cropped).jpg.

■ CHAPTER 5

Social Stratification

The year was 2081, and everybody was finally equal. They weren't only equal before God and the law. They were equal every which way. Nobody was smarter than anybody else. Nobody was better looking than anybody else. Nobody was stronger or quick than anybody else.
– Kurt Vonnegut, *Harrison Bergeron*

This is an excerpt from the first paragraph of Kurt Vonnegut's short story *Harrison Bergeron* (1961). Although the story is fiction, it provides a lens through which we can imagine a society free of social hierarchies. In the story, the government goes to great lengths to impose social standardization, such as contrived physical handicaps and electric shock. The image of the main character from the story displays Harrison wearing all of his mandated handicaps in order to ensure true equality and disallow any individual from being smarter, stronger, or more attractive than anyone else. This tragic satire shows us what a world could look like if

Image 5.1

equality was about lowering everyone to the same level. However, most who look for ways to generate equality in our society try to do so by ensuring those born with disadvantages have the same opportunities as those who are more advantaged, wishing to lift everyone up to the same level.

It is impossible to completely remove the unique attributes of human beings. In every society for as long as human life has been documented, there have been various arbitrary measures of distinction. Some civilizations have based it on heritage, others wealth, or even biological characteristics. These divisions become a part of the social structure through the institutionalization of laws and policies and visual depictions of difference transmitted through the media. Consequently, not only are physical features believed to imply behavioral characteristics, differences in the social outcomes of people's lives are seen as natural instead of socially constructions.

Differences among people become distinct classifications that determine opportunities for social mobility, access to resources, and social regard. Thus, a system of inequality is formed in which one's economic standing, gender, sexual orientation, religion, race, ethnicity, or age shapes their life chances. These social attributions in turn influence one's life expectancy, insurance coverage, educational attainment, and the ability to move freely and safely in the world. Social inequality not only has implications in the day-to-day lives of individuals, but also extends to global relationships. In the United States, the "American Dream" is far from the grasp of many of its residents. It is not because they are not hardworking or because they are incompetent. It is largely because of the fact that only a select share of the population has been granted wealth, authority, and influence. The systemic barriers to individual and collective social mobility are given less attention than the centering of individual responsibility narratives. A sociological analysis of stratification involves examining it as a social system reinforced by cultural ideologies. It is through this lens that we will examine social stratification in this chapter.

✔ CHAPTER OBJECTIVES

After completing this chapter students should be able to do the following:

✔ **Distinguish** slavery, caste, and class systems of stratification.

✔ **Define** *socioeconomic status* and discuss its influence on one's life chances.

✔ **Explain** the various factors that influence one's life chances.

✔ **Discuss** the role of cultural capital in one's social mobility.

✔ **Discuss** three key facts about global stratification.

✔ **Explain** one of the current proposals to address global equity and one alternative approaches to global equity.

KEY TERMS

social stratification

social class

income

wealth

social mobility

cultural capital

intragenerational social

mobility

intergenerational social

mobility

world systems theory

neocolonialism

imperialism

equity literacy

SYSTEMS OF STRATIFICATION

"It's not fair!" is an expression that we have either heard or used at one point or another in our lifetime. This expression has been used in response to perceived slights or in recognition of wrongdoing by someone or something. It is through cultural socialization that we learn to recognize and distinguish what is "right" or "wrong," "fair" and "unfair." Although humans notice differences and distinctions among one another at a young age, for most people a deeper analysis of inequality comes later in life through years of schooling and life experiences.

Social stratification can be defined as the ranking of entire groups of people into a hierarchy in which those at the top are rewarded most and have higher social regard. It is important to highlight that social stratification involves *entire groups*, not just individuals. The cultural and even legal classification of individuals into various social groups that are defined by dominant cultural ideologies assists the process of social stratification as it provides ideas about the proper social placement of individuals. We come to believe that it is individual choices and actions that determine a person's success in life. While there is certainly a role played by individual actors in the fashioning of their lives, we cannot ignore the larger social structure and external forces that shape and mold individual circumstances.

Slavery

One of the oldest and most enduring systems of social stratification is slavery. In North America, there were 2 centuries of chattel slavery in which Africans were taken from the continent and forced to work without pay or dignity. The enslaved were stripped of all of their civil and human rights and worked literally to death in many cases. Families were separated, learning to read and write was prohibited, and any children born from an enslaved person was also deemed a slave. Unlike indentured servitude and convict leasing, there was no end in sight once a person was enslaved; it was a life-long, permanently ensconced status. According to the Trans-Atlantic Slave Trade Database, 12.5 million Africans were shipped to the so-called "New World," in which less than 400,000 were brought to North America. Although the enslavement of Africans was carried out in different modes and forms throughout the Americas, Caribbean, and Latin America, they all share the characteristics of forced enslavement and the buying and selling of human beings.

It is commonly believed that chattel slavery has been abolished, but other forms of forced labor have emerged in its place in the form of debt peonage, sex trafficking, organ trafficking, and child exploitation. The International Labor Organization (2017) reported that about 24.9 million people throughout the world are forced laborers in these sectors, most of which are women and girls.

Caste Systems

Caste systems, which exist in some societies today, such as parts of India, Nepal, and Sri Lanka, are stratification systems in which people are categorized and placed into a social hierarchy upon birth. It has been debated whether caste determinations are influenced by racial characteristics such as skin color or broader political and economic considerations. Caste relegations can determine whom an individual can marry, what type of work they do, or even where they live in a community. Like other systems of inequality, those on the higher tier of the social strata believe themselves to be superior in morals, intelligence, capacity, and other traits than those who occupy the lower tiers. Caste systems resemble the system of chattel slavery in that people are locked into their caste with little possibility of change.

Social Class Systems

Although it can be argued that racism in the United States has produced caste-like outcomes for Black Americans and other oppressed ethnic groups, it is **social class** that is the fundamental basis of the U.S. stratification system. Social classes are groups of people who share a similar economic position in society based on their income and wealth. Therefore, the social class stratification system is economic. While job employment offers an opportunity to generate income (at varying amounts), wealth is much harder to come by. **Wealth** refers to the combined value of a person's income and other material assets such as real estate and stocks. **Income** is the money a person earns through salary or wages. Currently about 10% of the richest people in the United States own almost 70% of the country's total wealth (Statista, 2021). Unlike income, wealth has capital gain, meaning the value of assets such as stock investments increase in value over time and can be sold at top value. According to a 2021 Congressional Research Service report on income distribution in the United States, "Even if the distribution of wealth did not change in the future, the capital income generated from these assets (if positive) will contribute to future income inequality" (p. 42).

The ranking of groups in a social class hierarchy can determine their access to vital resources and their life chances in general. Although class systems of stratification have no legal barriers to **social mobility**, or the movement of people from one level to another, it is difficult if not impossible for some people to advance from the social class position in which they were born. Some economists predict that it would take five or six generations to erase the advantages or disadvantages of a person's economic beginnings.

CULTURAL CAPITAL

Along with monetary resources, or what Karl Max would call *capital*, **cultural capital** can also be stimuli for social mobility. Cultural capital was described by French theorist Pierre Bourdieu (1986) as the symbols, ideas, tastes, and preferences that can be strategically used as resources in a society. Bourdieu argued that cultural capital formed the foundation of social life and determined one's position within the social order. According to Bourdieu, cultural capital comes from three sources: embodied, objectified, and institutional capital. Cultural capital can be used for economic, social, or even political purposes. Nonmonetary forms of cultural capital often provide avenues for economic and material advancement. Inequity exists in the social value of certain forms of cultural capital over another. For example, **institutionalized capital** refers to technical and educational qualifications and credentials. In a capitalist and highly bureaucratic country like the United States, institutionalized capital can be incredibly valuable for social advancement. In countries that are governed by religious principles, such as Indonesia, **embodied capital**, which refers to one's personality, character, and behavior, may be more beneficial. **Objectified capital** refers to cultural goods like one's possessions, art, and other material objects. Objectified capital is often understood as a symbol of one's economic standing but can also be used to generate income and wealth.

Embodied Capital

Pierre Bourdieu (1986) argued that embodied capital was a prerequisite to other forms of capital. Additionally, embodied capital, according to Bourdieu, is used to appropriate other forms of capital by the owners of the means of production. Celebrities and public figures are examples of groups who positively benefit from embodied capital. Some may argue that it is the objectified capital of celebrities that captures the attention and envy of the masses. This would not be incorrect. However, many of these individuals are also large "personalities" with charisma that pique the interest of audiences. At times embodied characteristics, such as a nice sense of humor, are more significant to admirers than one's level of talent or any credentials that they may have.

Objectified Capital

We certainly cannot underestimate the significance of objectified capital in a world where what you have is so often linked to perceptions about who you are. Many of the aspirations that make up the so-called "American dream" are objectifications. For example, buying a house is one pillar of the American dream ideology. A home is obviously objectified capital, which is used to indicate one's social status and class mobility. Objectified capital is assumed to symbolize a person's efforts and subsequent success. This capital engenders confidence in the work ethic and productivity of individuals, making them even more attractive and sought after, therefore leading to even more "success."

Institutionalized Capital

While technical and academic credentials are put forward as primary components to success in the United States, embodied and objectified capital blur the significance of institutionalized capital. In contemporary American society it is not only *what* you know, but very much *who* you know that can influence social advancement. The value of a college education seems to be diminishing over time, yet higher education is still being promoted as the key to landing a good work (Vedder & Strehle, 2017). In reality, job markets are oversaturated with individuals holding college degrees. Many quality jobs in today's world do not require college degrees due to the technical skills that are central to many science and technology occupations. This is not to say that a college education has no value. Those with higher levels of education are less likely to be unemployed for long periods and are far less likely to be impoverished. However, in a knowledge economy, creative individuals are launching businesses and building substantial online platforms having never gone to college.

SOCIAL MOBILITY

In a primarily class-based system like that of the United States, there is potential for individuals to mobilize or move about the social spectrum. Of course, variables such as income level, gender, race, ethnicity, marital status have powerful influence on the extent to which this is possible. Social mobility can be *upward* or *downward* for both individuals and societies. Entire countries can experience structural social mobility through economic and technological advancement. However, upward structural social mobility does not always equate to elevating the lives and statuses of individuals within a society.

Intragenerational social mobility can be defined as a change in social position occurring during a person's lifetime. **Intergenerational social mobility** refers to the upward or downward social mobility of children in relation to their parents. Research on social mobility in the latter half of the 20th century and the early 21st century generally concluded that upward social mobility in the United States was fairly high, though uneven, and small within single generations (Macionis, 2008). Social welfare professor Mark R. Rank and economics professor Lawrence E. Eppard, argue that today the "ladder of opportunity" has become much harder to climb in the United States largely due to increasing levels of income and wealth inequality. They note that the United States has far less mobility and equality of opportunity today than the European Union or other OECD (Organization for Economic Co-operation and Development) countries. A couple of reasons provided are the lack of significant investment in social welfare and efforts to remedy structural inequities (Rank & Leppard, 2021).

China, a country of over 1.4 billion inhabitants, has managed to lift nearly 800 million people out of poverty, achieving the complete elimination of extreme poverty. This contributed to more than 70% of global poverty reduction! The socialist government of China, currently under the leadership of Xi Jinping, has named inadequate development as the root cause of poverty. This unprecedented reduction in poverty was accomplished through a collaborate and systemic effort that included identifying the low income, generating a low income–centered philosophy, and social welfare investments totaling nearly 1.6 trillion yuan. This equates to 244 billion U.S. dollars (Jiang et. al., 2021; June, 2021).

GLOBAL STRATIFICATION AND WORLD SYSTEMS THEORY

Stratification is a micro and macro phenomenon, shaping and impacting individuals, groups, cities, states, countries, and the entire world. One of the best explanations of global stratification comes from the **world systems theory** developed by sociologist Immanuel Wallerstein. Wallerstein (2008) used a "capitalist world economy" model to illustrate a global economic hierarchy in which powerful and resourced countries were in the top tiers and poorer countries were at the bottom and dependent on the affluent nations. His analysis of the global economy traces back

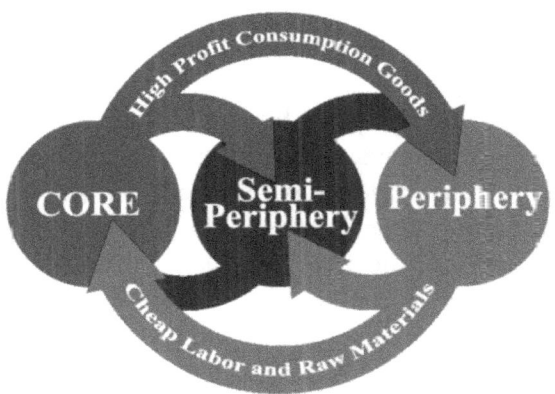

Wallerstein's World System Theory Model

Image 5.2

more than 500 years, beginning with the European colonization of parts of Asia, most of Africa, and the Americas, leading to an unprecedented accumulation of wealth and control of land and resources.

According to Wallerstein's global stratification model, wealthy nations are the core of the world economy. These countries are central because raw materials from around the world were funneled first to western Europe and today are additionally channeled to North America, Australia, and Japan. Low-income nations were identified as the *periphery* of the world economy. Their introduction into the world economy was through colonial exploitation, and today they continue to support wealthier countries through raw materials and inexpensive labor. The remaining countries are classified as the *semi-periphery* of the world economy. These nations are considered middle-income and have attributes of both core and periphery countries. The economic and political dominance of more industrialized and wealthy nations over nations with less illustrate what is referred to as **neocolonialism**. One way neocolonialism is exhibited today is through the practice of wealthy nations selling low-income countries goods—especially weapons—on credit, creating a circle of debt and dependency (Henslin, 2015).

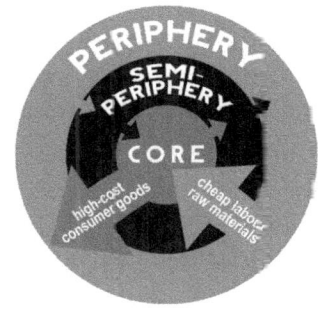

Image 5.3

The world has changed quite a bit since Wallerstein's theory of the world system. Although the continents of Europe and North America remain the most industrialized and structurally developed in the world, some countries have become highly productive and can no longer be considered semi-periphery (i.e., China, Norway, South Africa).

There have also been new conceptions about what "development" and "resources" mean. Historian Walter Rodney (1972) writes in his landmark book *How Europe Underdeveloped Africa* that development occurs on the individual, group, and societal level. Rodney states that development is a social process that is transient; all phases of development eventually give way to something else. He further argues that capitalism hinders human social development due to the dependency and exploitation that characterizes it. Rodney was heavily influenced by the economic analysis of Karl Marx and Frederick Engels (1848), who posited that capitalism would eventually see its demise and communism would replace it. Russian revolutionary Vladimir Lenin, in his 1916 paper, *Imperialism, the Highest State of Capitalism*, defines **imperialism** as (a) a concentration of production and monopolies, (b) banking/finance capital oligarchy, (c) the export of capital, (d) the division of the world among capitalist associations, and (e) the division of the world among powers. Obviously, capitalism has not yet seen its end, but even a brief examination of the world today would reveal Lenin's components of imperialism, most notably global financial organizations such as the World Bank and the International Monetary Fund.

It is important to keep in mind that geography and land borders are social constructions. Those with the power and authority to do so have been able to name land masses, divide territories, and establish borders. Counter-mapping projects offer keen insight into the ways geography aids in the development of ideologies about land and people and often reinforce status quo power structures. Furthermore, notions of development are heavily influenced by geopolitical considerations. For example, in 2020 the U.S. government made changes in the way that it would conduct aspects of its trade remedy investigations, which are established to purportedly protect domestic industries from being negatively impacted by imports and/or unfair trading practices. In turn, the United States updated the rules and criteria it uses for designating a country as *developed*, generating a new status for South Africa as a *developed* country (Naumann, 2020).

Continuous trends in economic progress and polarization require frequently revisiting the views of all world systems, modernization, and dependency theories. The dire outcomes of capitalism have ignited more interest in socialism and the need for economic and political redistribution within and outside of the United States. The gulf between the world's wealthy and the world's low income and the systems and practices that generate and maintain this gulf have led to remarkable climate catastrophe, mass displacement, and increased war and conflict. It seems that the only way to achieve a peaceful and wholesome world is through transformation aimed at resolving social and systemic inequalities.

RETHINKING APPROACHES TO EQUITY

As the world continues to change and evolve, approaches to equity should follow suit. The invention and continual development of information communication technologies have uncovered the stories, experiences, and perspectives of people all over the world. Contributions from the most marginalized individuals across societies sometimes provide some of the keenest insights into how to address social problems and the disparities of stratification. When we draw from Rodney's definition of *development*, we include individual and small social group development. We therefore factor things such cultural and intellectual development into the equation. Many countries that are not the most economically affluent are quite rich in culture and innovation. Take Cuba for example, a country that has developed five different COVID-19 vaccines to date, a vanguard diabetes treatment program, and average life expectancy rates higher than that of the United States, all while enduring 60 years of embargo from the United States (Beaubien, 2022).

All sorts of interesting and innovative ideas have come from organizations seeking to address disparities in education, science, and technology. The Equity Literacy Institute (2021), defines equity literacy as

> **Equity literacy** is a comprehensive approach for creating and sustaining equitable schools. The foundations of equity literacy are (1) a commitment to deepening individual and institutional understandings of how equity and inequity operate in organizations and societies, and (2) the individual and institutional knowledge, skills, and will vigilantly identify inequities, eliminate inequities, and actively cultivating equity. At the individual level, when we embrace equity literacy, we learn to become a *threat to the existence of inequity* and an active *cultivator of equity* in our spheres of influence (p. 1).

Beyond educational rethinking of equity, some have even considered things like edible insects as a solution to world hunger (*The Economist*, 2022). Imagination and experimentation are what has always brought about transformative change and our current historical epoch requires the same. A critical lens and analysis should be implemented in any strategy to cultivate balance and equity to ensure that we are not creating new forms of social inequality and environmental degradation.

Applying Sociology: The World's Billionaires

According to the Forbes World Billionaires 2022 list, there are 2,668 billionaires in the world worth a collective $12.7 trillion. Most reign from the United States, which consists of 735 billionaires worth a collective $4.7 trillion. The 20 richest Americans have more wealth than all 160 million Americans in the economic bottom half of the U.S. population (Henslin, 2019).

Sociologists measure social class, or socioeconomic status by using income, education, and occupational prestige. However, many of the world's millionaires and billionaires do not hold college degrees and may not hold occupations that are particularly "prestigious." Sociologist Max Weber's (1948) theory of stratification included *power* as a dimension of one's social class position. Weber defined *power* as the probability that someone could exercise their will, even in the face of resistance. Power and influence are notable characteristics of the world's richest people. These individuals have unique access to key politicians, own the largest media and entertainment outlets, and have significant influence on the boards of major colleges and universities.

Do you believe that anyone should have billions of dollars? What would you do with such money? Would you share your wealth to those in need? Although there are worthy criticisms about the investments and development projects funded by the world's fourth wealthiest person, Bill Gates, he has also donated an estimated $36 billion to "charitable causes," more than any other billionaire or otherwise documented in human history (Reuters, 2021).

1. How would the world's billionaires be analyzed from a *functionalist* perspective?
2. How would the world's billionaires be analyzed from a *conflict* perspective?
3. How would the world's billionaires be analyzed from a *symbolic interaction* perspective?
4. How would the world's billionaires be analyzed from a *feminist* perspective?

SUMMARY: CONNECTING THE PIECES

Although social stratification may indeed be an inevitable aspect of any human society, the extent to which it occurs is dependent on social, economic, and political structures and ideologies. Variables such as race, ethnicity, social class, gender, and education shape opportunities and disadvantages the world over. One's position on the social hierarchy can have implications for access to resources, social mobility, and even life expectancy. It is for these reasons that social stratification should be identified and addressed in all efforts to bring forth balance, justice, and progressive development. It is also important to acknowledge the global stratification system that is shaped and maneuvered by the world's most powerful and wealthy countries. Conceptions about development, progress, and democracy are centered around the values and norms of these countries. However, development extends beyond the economy. Political, cultural, social, and individual development are equally important for societies striving to be inclusive, egalitarian, and advancing. Scientific, technological, and industrial advancements should be partnered with humanistic development that never ignores the plight of masses of people, for it is only by lifting those at the bottom rungs and margins of society elevate and stabilize the entire society.

REVIEW AND CRITICAL THINKING

Directions: Respond to the questions and prompts, based on what you have learned in this chapter:

1. Distinguish among slavery, caste, and class systems of stratification. In what ways are elements of caste and class present in the social system of the United States?
2. Describe the different types of cultural capital and their advantages.
3. Discuss social mobility in the United States. What factors influence one's options for social mobility?
4. Describe how China was able to eliminate extreme poverty.
5. Describe world systems theory and how the model has evolved over time.
6. Distinguish between the terms *neocolonialism* and *imperialism*.
7. Discuss some of the modern approaches to equity.
8. Note one fact about the world's billionaires.

Credits
IMG 5.1: Source: https://discover.hubpages.com/politics/Harrison-Bergeron-Is-The-Quest-For-Equality-Always-Fair.
IMG 5.2a: Kendall Moyer, https://medium.com/@kendallgrace15/periphery-role-in-the-world-systems-theory-fa5d291cac55. Copyright © 2016 by Kendall Moyer.
IMG 5.2b: Mirkyton, https://commons.wikimedia.org/wiki/File:Wallerstein%27s_Core-periphery_model.png, 2021.

■ CHAPTER 6

Gender

NBA athlete Dwayne Wade and his wife, actress Gabrielle Union, made headline news when they shared that their child, named Zion at birth, and given the sex-assignment of boy, decided to live as a girl and be called Zaya. Zaya's parents are very supportive of her

Image 6.1

decision and have spoken about seeking advice from trans-identifying individuals and researching the subject in depth. However, they have received extreme backlash from peers, strangers online, and several public figures. Comments have ranged from them being inadequate parents to the child needing intense therapy. Many have regurgitated statements uttered often over the years such as Zaya being too young to understand her identity or the perception that U.S society encourages children to be gay. These comments reveal the consistent and erroneous connection between one's gender identity and one's sexual identity. Social scientists and medical doctors have confirmed that human brain and body development do not always align (Mascarelli, 2015). There is no concrete connection between one's assigned sex, their gender, or their sexual orientation. Yet this narrative is maintained in mainstream U.S. culture. Presumably, some of these individuals would prefer that Wade and Union kick their child out of the home and disclaim her from the family. This is exactly what happens to many LGBT+ youth who currently make up the largest portion of homeless youth in the United States. They also experience higher rates of bullying and suicide as compared to their non-LGBT+ counterparts. For years, trans individuals, some of whom are writers and activists, have stated that they were indeed "born this way" and that they have always felt out of place in the body that they were born into and/or the gender category they were assigned. Justifying their oppression and mistreatment also justifies the oppression and mistreatment of other less dominant groups who were born with a certain skin color or in a certain place in the world.

✓ CHAPTER OBJECTIVES

After completing this chapter students should be able to do the following:

✔ **Distinguish** between sex and gender.

✔ **Discuss** the extent to which one's gender identity influences their life chances and experiences.

✔ **Describe** the specific ways that women are the targets of physical and sexual violence in the United States and abroad.

✔ **Identify** the ways gender differences are institutionalized and embedded into the social structure.

✔ **Describe** "doing gender" and how gender is performed on a daily basis.

✔ **Provide** an analysis of feminism, its strengths and weaknesses.

KEY TERMS

sex	gender roles	femicide
gender	cisgender	feminism
gender binary	hidden curriculum	patriarchy
intersex	motherhood penalty	
gender rules	rape culture	

THE GENDER BINARY

The term *binary* refers to a system with two, and only two, distinct and separate parts. Therefore, a **gender binary** is the idea that there are only two types of humans—one that is male bodied and masculine and one that is female bodied and feminine. The term **sex** is used to refer to physical differences in primary sexual characteristics, such as reproductive organs, and secondary sexual characteristics, such as breast tissue and facial hair (Wade & Ferree, 2019). The belief around the gender binary is the that two body "types" are opposite, contrasting, and distinct. However, a scientific and biological analysis shows that the idea of "opposite sexes" may not be completely accurate either. According to professors and authors Lisa Wade and Myra Marx Ferree in their textbook *Gender: Ideas, Interactions, Institutions* (2019),

> The penis and scrotum *do* have something in common with female anatomy. The same tissue that becomes the scrotum in in males becomes the outer labia in females; the penis and clitoris are formed of the same erectile tissue and clustered nerve endings; and testes and ovaries are both gonads that make germ cells (sperm and eggs), one just a modified version of the other. (p. 10)

There also exists the collective assumption that each sex category is homogeneous—that individuals think, live, and behave in the same ways. Anyone who is aware and consciously living in the 21st century can witness the contradictions to this binary by our lived experiences. We know or have learned of people who identify as *queer, transgender, intersex,* and otherwise nonbinary. Regardless of whether one believes in multiple sexes or a gender spectrum, we cannot deny this reality. Even bodies are not homogeneous, even when given the same sex classification. It is estimated that between one in 1,500–2,000 people are **intersex**, meaning that they were born with reproductive or sexual anatomy that doesn't fit the standard definitions of female or male. If one's cells lack the ability to detect hormones such as androgen or testosterone, one can have the body plan of a "male" or "female" but not their associated reproductive organs (i.e., testes, ovaries) or tissue that grows together in the same organ. So, instead of the standard XY male sex assignment and XX female sex assignment, an intersexed person may have X or XXY chromosomes (Intersex Human Rights Australia [IHRA], 2013, King, 2015). Intersex classifications are a reminder that so-called male and female bodies are not as straightforward as we may think. Therefore, **gender** is a better way of describing the sense of self and expression that individuals embody and portray. Gender is both the personal traits that an individual possesses, along with a dimension of social organization and interaction.

It is important to consider how narratives about sex and gender are formed and transmitted in a society. Each of the religious texts of the Abrahamic religion's Judaism, Christianity, and Islam describe the story of creation. The first chapter of the Bible, Genesis, describes the creations of humans, stating that God made man on the 6th day of creation, fashioned him in His own image, and gave him dominion over the rest of creation. The Book of Genesis in the Hebrew bible (Torah) contains a second narrative in which Adam and Eve are not named; instead, it says that God created *humankind* in His image. In the Holy Qur'an, both Adam and Eve transgress by eating from the forbidden tree, both are held responsible, and both are shown mercy and forgiveness by God. According to Amina Wadud in *Qur'an and Woman* (1999), "Although the male and female essential contingent characters in the creation of humankind, no specific cultural functions or roles are defined at the moment of creation" (p. 26). The creation narrative bestowed from these dominant religions is central to the gender binary narrative in which humanity is believed to be derived from a single pair of original ancestors. The biblical notion of "original sin" is also important in the shaping of the gender binary. Eating from the forbidden tree is viewed by Christians as the original sin. According to the teachings of many religions, deviations from standard sexual and gender identities are viewed as "unholy." Additionally, any romantic partnership that deviates from this standard is seen as an abrasion to sexuality and gender norms.

DOING GENDER AND GENDER MAINTENANCE

Since gender is constructed and given meaning through psychological, social, and cultural means, it requires maintenance to be sustained. Candace West and Don Zimmerman (1987) coined the phrase *doing gender* to describe the complex interactional nature of gender that emerges from social situations "both as an outcome of and a rationale for various social arrangements and as a means of legitimating one of the most fundamental divisions of society" (p. 3). Doing gender involves much more than the way one dresses or how they style their hair. Although that is a part of it, doing gender is involves both gender displays, gender roles, and gendered social arrangements. Doing gender includes sometimes conforming to and sometimes breaking "gender rules." **Gender rules** are instructions about how to appear and behave as a "man" or "woman." Gender rules shape the expectations for behavior of individuals or **gender roles** of individuals assigned to particular categories. However, gender rules vary by culture, history, and social context. They are further complicated by other aspects of one's identity such as social class, race and ethnicity, or religion. Gender rules are embedded into the process of socialization that begins in infancy. Differentiating between the voices of individuals, "girl toys" versus "boy toys," preferred clothing colors, and ideal play partners are things that children as young as 2 years have internalized. Of course, households vary in their levels of gender conformity or defiance, but little variation is accepted in practice in the major institutions of society. Therefore, our experiences in the public realm are largely shaped by a gender binary framework.

One may think, "Well, if you don't agree with a gender binary, then just live your personal life differently." That is much easier said than done! In a society that is shaped and oriented by notions of a gender binary, individuals may find it much easier to just "go along to get along." However, this can cause much psychological tension and trauma for people who do not feel as though they are their true selves. Additionally, there are various levels of reaction to gender rule defiance. In some cases, the reaction to a perceived "boy" wearing eye shadow and eye liner is a dirty look from a stranger. In other cases, this same individual may be harassed, physically assaulted, or worse. In the United States, transgender (particularly transwomen and trans-feminine people) and nonbinary individuals endure sexual violence, physical violence, and homicide at higher rates than **cisgender** individuals, or those whose gender identity corresponds in a socially favorable way to their sex assigned at birth (American Civil Liberties Union [ACLU], 2020). Decisions about how and whether to follow gender rules have real social consequences and outcomes. How much of a role, if any, should social institutions and general members of a society have on the choices that individuals make for themselves and their intimate persons? This is one of many questions that we will continue to grapple with as perceptions and practices of gender shift and change over time and space.

GENDERED INSTITUTIONS

Gendered perceptions and practices are given place and meaning within the social institutions of society. Like race, ethnicity, and age, gender is given magnitude through its significance at the macro and micro levels. Aside from the gendered labeling of many public restrooms, most social spaces are not outrightly segregated by gender. However, one only needs to take a brief walk around a college campus, workplace, or shopping mall to notice the pervasiveness of gender homogeneous friend groups, and more often than not, heterosexual romantic pairings. These are self-selections, not enforced by law or policy (in the United States). After years of gender socialization and the normalization of gender rules and roles in domestic and public realms, people begin to fall in line. We begin to think that these are choices that we have made for ourselves and may not even recognize our daily gender performances. The unconscious and mechanical ways in which we engage in gender expression fortifies its construction—namely because we begin to think of it as innate and natural instead of learned.

Education

One major form of social mobility in life is to obtain an education. Most countries have compulsory education, which refers to a period of education required of all people in a society by the government. Throughout history and to the present day there is great variation throughout the world in educational access and opportunities along gender lines. Although most people will have a point of connection with the education institution at some time in their lives, completion of degrees and educational outcomes are disparate categorically.

Functionalist theorists would note how schools have the responsibility of socializing children. It is within schools that young people undergo several hours a day learning "their place" in not only the classroom and school, but the larger society as well. Not only are formal curriculums layered with gender bias, stereotyping, and patriarchy, but **hidden curriculum**, the unwritten rules and behavioral expectations of a school system, operate simultaneously to convey dominate social expectations of gender, among many other things. From a functionalist viewpoint, schools work to establish a common value system among diverse members of a society. Unfortunately, numerous research studies have indicated that schools reproduce the social inequalities reflected in the larger society. Gendered inequities are no exception to this. Stereotypes about the "assertive male" and "passive female" permeate school classrooms as female students become increasingly quieter in class as they progress through grade levels (Alber, 2017). The crystallization of gender norms may be one explanation for this, but educators also bear responsibility. Researchers David Sadker and Karen Zittleman describe their classroom observations in public and private schools over the course of several years in their book *Still Failing at Fairness: How Gender Bias Cheats Girls and Boys in School and What We Can Do About It* (2010). The authors note that starting in grade school, teachers that they observed engaged less frequently with female students while at the same time providing males with more feedback. Teacher time, energy, and attention leaned heavily in favor of male students. As individuals progress through education, they begin to choose classes and career paths that align with dominant gender expectations. There are numerous initiatives currently taking place in the United States to encourage girls, women, and marginalized groups to pursue activities and careers in STEM (science, technology, engineering, mathematics) fields that have been overwhelmingly occupied by White males. A recent study conducted at the University of Michigan confirmed that "White, heterosexual men without disabilities are privileged in STEM careers" (Wadley, 2022, para. 1). Careers within these areas also tend to be some of the most prestigious and highly paid occupations, contributing to the ongoing gender-wage gap.

Workplace

Let's begin this section on the gendered nature of work by first disavowing from the notion that paid work is the only valuable and legitimate form of work. Caregivers and parents who are not employed outside of the home are also engaging in meaningful and essential work. Economic frameworks such as that of capitalism tether work to income earned from a social institution. Since the economic values of a society are transmitted and reinforced through culture, we learn through socialization to aspire to work for money. Additionally, this socialization is gendered by situating men as ideal workers and family breadwinners. This is one way to explain why men are more likely to engage in paid work than women.

As mentioned in the previous section, education and skill accumulation is a general mandate for gainful employment. Countries like Afghanistan, Pakistan, and Guinea, among others, have significant barriers or restrictions on the education of girls and women, which inevitably leads to their low levels of employment. Of course, we must also account for the political instability and economic recession of these countries. However, degrees alone have not balanced the unequal pay between men and women in places like the United States. According to a Pew Research Center analysis in 2020, women earned 84% of what men earned based on median hourly earnings of both full- and part-time workers. The wage gap was smaller for women workers ages 25 to 34 than for all workers 16 and older. Women workers ages 25 to 34 earned 93 cents for every dollar a man in the same age group earned on average. Pay depends largely on the occupational field in which one is employed, and women are still overrepresented in so-called "pink-collar" jobs, or care-oriented fields that historically have been considered women's work. According to the U.S. Bureau of Labor Statistics 2021 report, women make up 80.5% of elementary and middle school teachers but only 21.9% of chief executives.

On the micro level, women workers endure discrimination, sexual objectification, and sexual harassment at much higher rates than men workers. Although the Civil Rights Act of 1964 made it illegal to discriminate based on gender, it is extremely difficult to show "proof" of discrimination and its consequences in courts that ask for evidence of things like intent, which may be nearly impossible to obtain. For instance, how can one "prove" that an employer discriminated against them based on pregnancy if the employer had not explicitly stated it in a documented form even though a **motherhood penalty**, or loss in wages per hour on the job associated with becoming a mother, has been well documented in research (American Association of University Women [AAUW], 2022).

The #MeToo movement that emerged in social media in 2006 has magnified patterns of sexual harassment and sexual abuse in ways unprecedented in the United States. Despite the fact that everyday women workers have endured sexual harassment and sexual abuse for some time, the high-profile nature of many of the #MeToo stories and cases captured the attention of the mass media in ways that others have not. Sadly, it took the experiences of celebrities to validate a trend of harm that has been generally overlooked for far too long.

Media

As stated in Chapter 3, a significant amount of daily life is spent consuming media—computers, smartphones, video games, podcasts, and so on. Countless hours of media consumption undoubtedly have an impact on how we conceptualize ourselves and our world. One of the most documented and consistent findings across gender categories and in all age and racial categories is that heavy consumption of entertainment media is strongly associated with adherence to stereotyped and traditional views about gender (Lindsey, 2016). On a micro level we may wave off the media's gender bias as a silly and inconsequential thing. However, the media is also a social institution in our society. As an institution, it contributes to the social devaluation of women and perpetuates gender inequalities. Depictions of women in the media are mainly produced by and for men. Here are some statistics on the control, creation, production, and dissemination of media images and information in the United States (Women's Media Center, 2021):

- Women own about 5.3% of the nation's 1,368 full-power commercial TV stations.
- Men host about 79% of the top podcasts, although women make up 50% of podcast listeners.
- Women of color filled 6% of executive roles in film and 9% in television.
- Women comprised 5% of experts in STEM who were mentioned and a third of persons quoted in 146,867 articles about COVID-19 that were published by 15 leading news organizations worldwide, including CNBC, CNN, Fox, *The New York Times*, and *USA Today*.
- No women aged 50 years and older were lead characters in the top 10 money-making films in the United States, United Kingdom, Germany, and France in 2019, according to the Geena Davis Institute on Gender in the Media.

Although there is evidence that suggests progress is being made in many areas of media representation, this must be converted to the real-life progress, success, and equity of all women.

Applying Sociology: Tests for Gender Representation and Equity in Media

Referred to as the Bechdel–Wallace test, any given work of fiction must (a) have at least two women in it, who (b) talk to each other about (c) something other than a man in order to pass. The test is a simple measure of gender representation and inequality in the media. The above graph shows how movies have improved representation over time, and how there are still a good amount of movies that don't meet the Bechdel-Wallace criteria for representation. While this test is not a perfect standard, it does establish decent guidelines in what can be expected as a baseline for women to be better represented and could be extrapolated and applied to other under-represented demographics.

According to bechdeltest.com, here is how a few popular films scored on the test:

Euphoria: 1 of 3

Scream: 3 of 3

Turning Red: 3 of 3

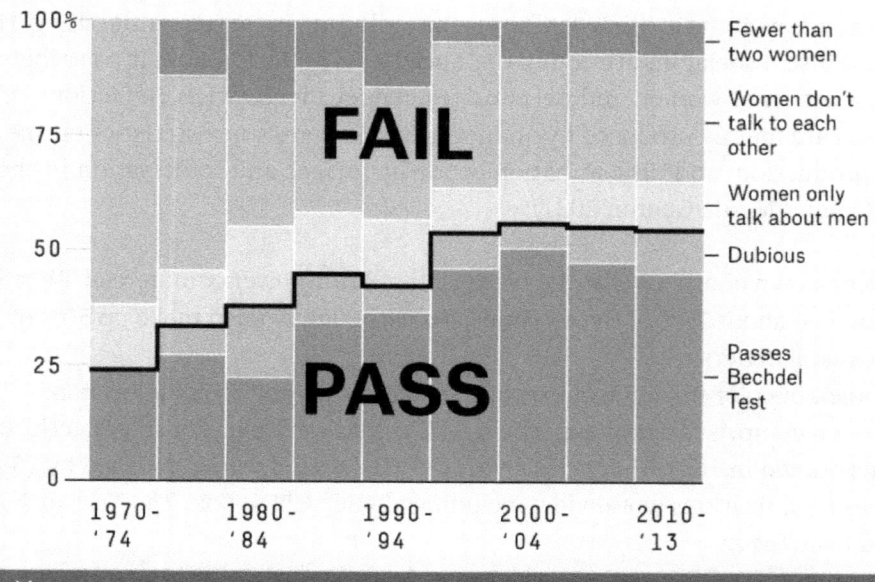

Image 6.2

GLAAD, the Gay & Lesbian Alliance Against Defamation, has introduced what they called "The Russo Test," named after GLAAD cofounder and film historian Vito Russo (Singer, 2013). It is designed to analyze how LGBTQ+ characters are represented in a fictional work. It evaluates movies based on three criteria:

- The film contains a character that is identifiably LGBT.
- That character must not be solely or predominantly defined by their sexual orientation or gender identity (i.e., the character is made up of the same sort of unique character traits commonly used to differentiate straight characters from one another).
- The LGBT character must be tied into the plot in such a way that their removal would have a significant effect, meaning they are not there to simply provide colorful commentary, paint urban authenticity, or (perhaps most commonly) set up a punchline; the character should matter.

Review at least three pieces of media (e.g., a show, movie, magazine) and apply both the Bechdel–Wallace test and the Russo test. Describe each of the three pieces of media that you reviewed and discuss the results of each test for each.

GENDERED VIOLENCE AND EXPLOITATION

Although great strides toward gender equity have been made in some parts of the world, women remain among the poorest groups in most societies around the world. The cultural devaluation of women translates to public devaluation, making women more vulnerable to abuse, violence, and exploitation. While this section will focus on physical and sexual violence, keep in mind that women are also more likely to be victims of international criminal enterprises such as human trafficking for both labor and sex (Newman, 2017). A globalized world economy has led to continual increases in these forms of international exploitation.

Rape

According to the National Sexual Violence Resource Center (2015), it is estimated that one in five women in the United States experienced completed or attempted rape during their lifetime. In most cases, rape is committed by relatives, partners, or acquaintances. Among college students, rape is most often committed by boyfriends, ex-boyfriends, or classmates. While television shows may lead one to believe that sexual violence is more likely to occur randomly by strangers, this is not supported by research findings. The rates of sexual violence against women provide some evidence of what Susan Brownmiller (1993) referred to as **rape culture**, a social context in which rape is prevalent and sexual violence against women is normalized and excused due to attitudes and norms that perpetuate the treatment of women as sexual objects and instill in men a sense of sexual entitlement.

Domestic Violence and Femicide

Not only do women experience sexual violence at much higher rates than men, but they are also more likely to be victims of domestic violence and murder by intimate partners. The term **femicide** is used to describe the intentional killing of women and girls, with gender being the main determinant. Various forms of femicide have spanned centuries, but not until recent years has public alarm, outrage, and advocacy been expressed on a global scale and garnered the attention of mainstream media. To illustrate the extent and lethality of gendered violence, we can examine the following statistics (ACLU, 2008; Lindsey, 2016; Newman, 2017; Violence Policy Center, 2020):

- Domestic violence is the leading cause of injury to women in the United States.
- Domestic violence is a primary cause of homelessness for women and families.
- Of all murder-suicides, 72% involve an intimate partner; 94% of the victims of these murder suicides are women.
- "Honor killings" of women who bring disgrace to their families is common in some parts of the world, including countries like Iran, Afghanistan, and Syria.

   In order to achieve gender balance and equity, a fundamental transformation of cultural values along with institutional patterns is required. This is a massive, but not impossible task. A resocialization process that does not starkly juxtapose individuals of different assigned sex categories is a good step in this process. This does not mean that we should attempt to erase all differences between people or shun those who find gender divides in their personal lives beneficial. However, we should interrogate the extent to which the personal views and choices of those who have the power to make decisions inform the policies, laws, and operations of social institutions. Furthermore, a cultural shift needs to occur that opposes and firmly sanctions all forms of abuse, violence, and subordination based on gender.

THE COMPLEXITIES OF FEMINISM

Feminism, once perceived as culturally taboo, has now become a common topic of conversation in mainstream media and among advocates and organizers for gender equity. Like critical race theory, it is poorly understood and widely misinterpreted. **Feminism** can be defined as a theory and practice of seeking to understand the position of women in a society relative to that of men and determine how to improve the treatment and status of those disparaged. What could be so taboo about that? Well, for those who desire to maintain dominance and authority over women and attribute femininity as secondary to masculinity, this can seem quite threatening. Furthermore, not every woman has been viewed or treated in the same way. What it means to be a woman and the opportunities and rights granted to those deemed women have varied considerably by race, ethnicity, and social class. This was poignantly illustrated by the formerly enslaved abolitionist Sojourner Truth's speech at the 1851 Women's Rights Convention where she asked the congregation "Ain't I a Woman?" forcing public recognition of the blatant differences in the ways in which White and Black women were treated.

Feminists have varying identities and ideologies that range from liberal to radical. For example, *liberal feminists* have the basic proposition that all people are equal and should not be denied opportunities or progress based on gender. For liberal feminists, the basic organization of society can be expanded to include egalitarian rights and opportunities of women. Liberal feminists tend to emphasize empowerment through personal achievement rather than collective struggle. Liberal feminism has been criticized as a White women-centered feminism aimed toward more privileged and resources women in a society. Contrarily, *socialist feminists* and *radical feminists* view capitalism as the main driver of the systemic dominance of men, or **patriarchy**, and disproportionate concentrations of wealth and power among the genders. They do not believe that reforms proposed by liberal feminists are adequate. For these feminists, only a socialist revolution that eliminates social class differences and previous conceptions of gender will resolve gender inequality.

Multicultural feminists draw our attention to the fact that women are not a monolith but distinct by social and cultural differences. Multicultural feminists note that the experiences of women vary greatly by race, ethnicity, social class, and region. Many of the organizers of the 2020 Women's March could be classified as multicultural feminists who set out to recognize the diversity of women in ways that had not been centered in prior marches. For instance, they prioritized the inclusion and accessibility of women of color, transwomen, and those with disabilities. For march organizers, a women's movement that does not include these individuals "is not a movement at all" (Brown, 2020, para. 7). Feminisms continue to emerge that further expand the diversity and representation of women and marginalized genders.

Decolonial feminists argue that gender is a colonial construct that emerged out of the historical colonization of the lands and resources of the Global South and Global East. For decolonial feminists, gender serves a political-economic function that delegates women of color, Black women, and Indigenous women as objects of labor and service to men and the international imperial order. Decolonial feminism recognizes these women as the subjects of historical and present-day struggles for decolonization, antipatriarchy, and all systems of dominance. According to feminist activist Pillar Villanueva (2019), "The most important aspect is that decolonial feminism is a plurality of experiences and agendas that fight against oppression, according to the needs of each territory and reality" (para. 21).

Feminism and feminist theories provide a space for negotiating the construction of gender and challenging structural arrangements, policies, and practices that sustain the dominance of men and masculine superiority. Gender equity is a long-term project of social transformation that is not unlike other struggles to upend the cultural, political, and economic hegemony of one group over others. A feminist perspective would necessitate the inclusion of gender equity into all progressive efforts and social movements aimed toward liberation from oppression, or as the Women's March organizers of 2020 proclaimed, "it is not a movement at all."

SUMMARY: CONNECTING THE PIECES

We began this chapter in a familiar place, examining gender as a binary consisting of two distinct sex classifications with equally distinct patterns of presentation and behavior. While it is true that there are differences in the anatomical makeup of those classified as male and female, these differences are subtle and can even overlap into intersex anatomies. Gender is not a sex classification. Gender is an expression of one's identity that may or may not be connected to their own or broader society's perception of their sex classification. Gender does not determine one's sexual orientation or sexual identity. Gender is a social construct that is given meaning and power through cultural ideologies and the practices and policies of social institutions. Gender requires maintenance and reinforcement to persist. We *do* gender in our daily lives and gender-ize media and other institutional spaces. Gender distinctions are functional for maintaining the traditional status quo, but they come with severe consequences for marginalized gender groups. The notion that men and masculinity are superior to other bodies and expressions has justified the exploitation and violence of those on lower tiers of the gender hierarchy. Feminism is one response aimed at countering and upending the patriarchy. It is not a perfect theory or practice but does provide a lens for critical analysis and a pathway for reimagining gender identities and gender relations. The goal of feminism is not to create a new hierarchy of dominance in which women and femininity are superior to men and masculinity. The goal of the most progressive feminists is to eliminate the hierarchy all together and allow individuals the ability to express a spectrum of gender identities without enduring discrimination and harm because of their choices.

REVIEW AND CRITICAL THINKING

Directions: Respond to the questions and prompts, based on what you have learned in this chapter:

1. Distinguish between sex and gender and describe how making them synonymous constructs a gender binary.
2. Describe how we "do gender" as individuals in everyday life. What challenges exist for individuals who "do" nonbinary and queer gender in public spaces?
3. Explain how dominant notions of gender are incorporated into social institutions.
4. How does gender stratification increase the likelihood of gendered violence and exploitation?
5. Define *feminism* and discuss different types of feminism.
6. Discuss some of the criticisms and praises of feminism.

Credits

IMG 6.1: Axelle, https://www.complex.com/pop-culture/zaya-wade-on-hateful-comments-after-coming-out-as-trans-trying-to-break-you. Copyright © 2022 by Bauer-Griffin, LLC.
IMG 6.2: Allison McCann, https://fivethirtyeight.com/features/the-dollar-and-cents-case-against-hollywoods-exclusion-of-women/. Copyright © 2014 by FiveThirtyEight.

■ CHAPTER 7

Race and Ethnicity

Although darker-skinned people, like those classified as Black, African, Asian, Brown, Arab, dual-heritage, or Indigenous, make up the majority of the world's population, they are considered "minority groups" in most places outside of the Global South. The use of the term *minority* facilitates the construction of majority/ minority paradigm in which the designated minority occupies a lower stratum of a society's social

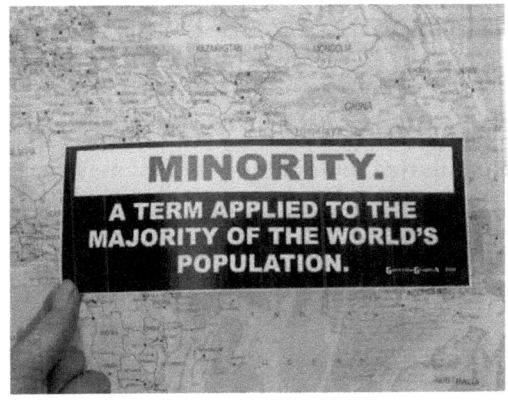

Image 7.1

and political hierarchy. Even a phrase such as "people of color" may not be as affirming as intended not only because it centers a White identity juxtaposed to an "other" identity, but it additionally conglomerates numerous ethnic groups with vast differences into a single category. Furthermore, the term is contextual to the United States and is not used or understood by many people abroad. Daniel Lim writes in his essay "I'm Embracing the Term 'People of the Global Majority'" (2020) that he prefers the term because

- it makes non-White people's identities independent of Whiteness
- it affirms non-White people's inherent power as the majority of the world's population
- it is inclusive of all non-White people around the world.

Increases in the world population have brought greater ethnic diversity than ever before. Superficial classifications of individuals and groups based on skin color or hair texture are subjective and arbitrary. However, these established ways of constructing race and ethnicity are still active in present throughout the world. Attempts should be made to further contextualize race and ethnicity and its intersections. In order to do so, we have to challenge the racism and political interests that have framed dominant racial narratives, discourse, practices, and policies. We can begin by examining the myths and realities regarding race and ethnicity.

✅ CHAPTER OBJECTIVES

After completing this chapter students should be able to do the following:

✔ **Contrast** the myths from the realities about race, ethnicity, and associated groups.

✔ **Discuss** changes in the construction of race over time and space.

✔ **Provide** examples of both cultural and institutional racism.

✔ **Explain** how racial and ethnic identity can shape political attitudes and choices.

✔ **Summarize** some of the antiracist movements and liberation struggles of the 21st century.

✔ **Recognize** the importance of slavery, colonization, and neocolonialism in constructing and maintaining race and racism.

KEY TERMS

biological determinism	ethnicity	discrimination
biological foundationalism	colorism	imperialism
race	prejudice	

MYTHS, ILLUSIONS, AND REALITY

In his book *The Groundings with My Brothers* (1969/2019) historian Walter Rodney writes,

> I'm putting it to my Black brothers and sisters that the color of our skin is the most fundamental thing about us. I could have chosen to talk about people of the same island, or the same religion, or the same class—but instead I have chosen skin color as essentially the most binding factor in our world. In so doing, I am not saying that is the way things ought to be. I am simply recognizing the real world—that is the way things are. Under different circumstances, it would have been nice to be color-blind, to choose my friends solely because

their social interests coincided with mine—but no conscious Black man can allow himself such luxuries in the contemporary world. (p. 2)

In this excerpt Rodney is acknowledging both the triviality of centering skin color in our understanding of humans and human behavior and the significance that skin color has within the social structure. Although **race** is a social construction in that its meaning was derived from human thought and interaction, it is also a reality. The observation that there are groups of people with inherited physical characteristics that distinguish them from other groups is a reality. Variations in **ethnicity**, or distinctive cultural characteristics, also exist. However, skin color is only skin deep. Human beings all over the world ae members of a single biological species that originated in Africa. Numerous scientific studies have revealed that genetic differences among human races are remarkably small (Aguirre & Turner, 2009; Feagin & Feagin, 2011; Gould, 1981; Lewontin, 1972). DNA research has revealed that most variation among human beings is within and not between so-called racial groups. Some common myths about race are that (a) there is a "pure race," (b) there are a fixed number of races, and (c) that inherent racial superiority exists. Although modern science has disavowed these myths (that it once constructed and supported), they are still operational throughout culture and within social institutions and are increasingly finding their way back into academic scholarship. The fact of the matter is that no system of racial classification can adequately account for the variety of physical traits that exist among humans. These physical differences are largely due to migration patterns throughout history. Every population of people has some genetic mixture, and this has only increased over time. Even though the concept of race is not biological, it does have real social implications. We will explore some of those implications later in this chapter.

Oyèrónkẹ́ Oyěwùmí (1997) argues in *The Invention of Women: Making an African Sense of Western Gender Discourses* that race, like gender, is a fundamental organizing principle in U.S. society. As an institutionalized concept, it can function regardless of the actions of individual people. It is the emphasis on **biological determinism**, which Oyěwùmí defines as the conception that biology provides the rationale for the organization of the social world, that shapes Western discourse on identity and social relations. Even when individuals, such as those who identify as feminists, attempt to make distinctions between the genetic and the socially constructed, **biological foundationalism** is still present. Therefore, if biology doesn't intrinsically determine social outcomes, it is still viewed as the foundation upon which experiences are drawn. Like sex and gender, race and ethnicity have not been able to escape the clenches of biological determinism in the West. However, this is not the case in all parts of the world. For example, Oyěwùmí writes that the Yoruba society of Southwestern Nigeria did not see the body as the basis for social classification. Instead, social hierarchies were determined by social relations, and individual social positions could shift depending on the situation. Ideologies and constructions of race vary around the globe, and even within the United States significant changes have transpired throughout its history.

CONSTRUCTIONS OF RACE ACROSS TIME AND SPACE

If we are to assert that race and ethnicity are social constructions, then we have to assume that there was a time in history when these terms did not exist in their modern sense. We also must consider that various constructions of race exist across time and space. Humans have made classifications by type, sort, and kind for likely as long as we have existed on earth. We know that caste systems existed in places like India long before modern racial systems were constructed. Although caste systems were based on heredity in some cases, skin color was not the primary factor of differentiation. Caste systems also differed from the modern racial system in that they were not based on a pseudo-scientific ideology of superiority and inferiority. It is difficult to determine exactly when the term *race* was developed, but we know that it was at least more than a century ago. In his essay "Race and History: Comments from an Epistemological Point of View," Staffan Müller-Wille (2014) traces the historiography of race to 18th-century European biological determinists like Carl Linnaeus (1735) who wrote the book *Systema Naturae* that classified humanity into four distinct racial categories—European, American, Asiatic, and African. Other scientists identified three racial types—*Caucasoid*, people with lighter skin and fine hair; *Negroid*, people with darker skin and course hair; and *Mongoloid*, people with yellow or brown skin and distinctive folds on the eyelids (Macionis, 2015). Each of these classifications presume a biologically "pure race." As stated earlier, we now know that there is more genetic variation within each of these categories than between them.

There is little significance in a biological view of race based on the revelations of contemporary research. However, as Oyěwùmí asserted, race is a foundational organizing principle of many societies. Racial distinctions justify social hierarchies that give some people more power and resources than others. These constructions can be quite extreme. A person would be classified as "colored" in many southern U.S. states throughout most of the 20th century if they were believed to even "one drop" of African blood or ancestry. This relegated entire populations of people to complete social, political, and economic disenfranchisement. Up until about 1950, Irish, Italian, and individuals of Jewish ancestry in the United States were considered "non-White" and therefore treated as subordinate members of society. In a country such as Brazil, we can see even more racial classifications: *branca* (White), *parda* (Brown), *morena* (brunette), *mulata* (mixed), *preta* (Black), or *amerela* (Yellow). What does it mean to be Black in a country like France that does not formally recognize or collect demographic data on race or ethnicity? The lack of acknowledgement of racial and ethnic diversity in France has not prevented racial discrimination or racial violence in the country.

Since 2000, the U.S. Census has allowed for individuals to choose more than one racial category. According to the 2020 U.S. Census report, 10.2% of respondents selected multiple races in the self-identification portion of the survey. This is an increase from 2.9% in 2010. Multiple race selections have had a greater increase in this time span than all single race selections. We can assume that there will continue to be an increase in individuals who identify with multiple races as U.S. population data predicts a continued numerical surge of marginalized racial groups and a "minority White" population by as early as 2045. Globally, it is predicted that by 2050 the population of Africa will double, making Africans one fourth (or 2.5 billion) of the world population (Paice, 2022). This information reinforces the fact that the possibilities for racial and ethnic categories are as endless as the variation of human species.

RACIAL AND ETHNIC STRATIFICATION

In the 21st century many people are asking why we have not yet been able to undo or deconstruct racism in our societies and around the world. One response to this question is that it would take considerable time and effort to deconstruct a system established centuries ago. that has been intricately woven into the social fabric of particularly multiracial societies. Another response to this question is that maintaining racism is in the interest of those who are able to enjoy elevated social stature and privileges due to their membership in the socially dominant group. Namely, it is European or White-identified peoples who benefit most from racialized systems. Every racialized social system contains components of **colorism**, prejudice, and discrimination based on skin shade and color. Individuals who have lighter skin shades are more positively regarded than those with darker skin tones. Colorism is both a collective social phenomenon and something that can be witnessed within ethnic groups. Like other forms of stratification, the tier that a group occupies on the social stratum has implications for social placement. Those on lower tiers of the stratification pyramid tend to have less power and resources within a society. These differences are justified through **prejudiced** cultural ideologies that generalize entire groups as less worthy and/or less capable of holding more significant social positions. Differential perceptions and unequal treatment, or **discrimination**, have also been institutionalized and coded into the laws, policies, and practices of social institutions.

Housing

According to the United Nations Human Rights Council, adequate housing is a fundamental human right, defining it as "the right to live somewhere in security, peace and dignity" (UNHRC, 2009, para. 22). Opinion polls indicate that this sentiment is shared by citizens of countries around the world. Not only does stable housing provide physical and psychological security for individuals, but it is also an indicator of the social conditions of a society. While homelessness is virtually nonexistent in socialist (and socialist-leaning) countries like Cuba and China, it continues to be one of the most significant social issues in capitalist countries. Finland recently introduced a "housing first" policy that entitled every citizen to a small apartment regardless of their mental health or financial standing. Homelessness has fallen tremendously since the implementation of this policy and continues to decline (Taggart, 2020). Countries such as South Africa, Scotland, and France have adopted a right to housing in their constitutions or legislation that has already reaped improvement in housing conditions (Solomon, 2020). However, right to housing laws are rare throughout the United States. Although individual states such as Massachusetts and New York City have implemented "right to shelter" policies that guarantee individuals a place in temporary shelters, this does not lead to secured housing. California, a state with a homeless population of over 108,000, is considering policies that would include amending the state constitution to create a legally enforceable mandate to provide housing for the unsheltered.

Marginalized ethnic groups experience homelessness at a disproportionate rate in the United States. For example, Black or African Americans make up 13% of the general population but 40% of the homeless population. Indigenous people across the United States continue to experience homelessness at even higher rates (U.S. Department of Housing and Urban Development [HUD], 2020). In order to understand racial discrimination in housing in the United States we have to look back at Federal Housing Administration policies after World War II. Beginning in the 1930s and 1940s, the federal government created subsidized loan programs that provided home ownership to millions of everyday U.S. citizens for the first time. Underwriters introduced a national appraisal system, linking property value and loan eligibility to race. As a result, communities that were entirely White received the highest ratings and marginalized ethnic groups and racially blended neighborhoods received the lowest ratings and were often denied these loans. Between 1934 and 1962, over $120 billion worth of new housing was subsidized by the government and less than 2% went to non-White families. Consequently, non-Whites were barred from home ownership. It wasn't until 1988 that fair housing laws were reformed to more strongly enforce antidiscrimination in home loan approvals (PBS, 2003). For decades White Americans were able to benefit from the security and equity provided by home ownership.

Health Care

Throughout the world, economic standing or class is correlated with health and health care. Data from numerous countries, including the United States, has shown that death rates and infant mortality rates are higher for people in the poorest 20% of the income distribution (Giddens, 2017). Marginalized racial groups, such as Black, Latino, and Indigenous populations, are more likely to not have health insurance, leading to disparate rates of illness, higher rates of infant mortality, and shorter life spans. Research studies have revealed many factors that contribute to health inequalities by race. In some cases, inequalities are attributed to the outright personal racism of health professionals. For example, one study concluded that doctors viewed Black Americans, regardless of income or education, as less intelligent, less likely to participate in rehabilitation, and less likely to follow medical advice. These prejudiced attitudes can (and do) shape the treatment decisions that doctors make, especially when resources are limited (Newman, 2017). To eliminate these disparities, we must not only address the obvious racism, but the income gap between the wealthy and the poor that directly impacts access to health care coverage and quality of treatment.

State-Sanctioned Violence

In the United States, nearly 1,000 people per year have been killed by police since 2013. Police are now a leading cause of death for young men in the United States, those between 20 and

25 years, and specifically young Black men. These murders are almost always systemically justified, resulting in less than 2% of police officer prosecutions (Lopez, 2021). Even vigilantes who murder Black people, ranging from community lynchings to neighborhood gunmen, tend to go unpunished. Some activists argue that mass incarceration is also a form of state-sanctioned violence. The United States is sometimes referred to as a "carceral state," one in which jail and prisons are the primary apparatus for dealing with deviance and crime. Of the over 2 million people in jail or prison throughout the country, over 38% are Black. Native or Indigenous people are even more overrepresented in the carceral system (2.8%) in relation to their overall percentage of the U.S. population, which is about 2% (Federal Bureau of Prisons, 2024).

RACIALIZED IMPERIALISM

According to Vladimir Lenin (1917), **imperialism** is the last stage of capitalism. This transition is brought about primarily through economic monopoly but includes geopolitical, social, and culture monopoly as well. The racial division of power, authority, and control over resources can be clearly seen on global, national, and local levels in most parts of the world. To reiterate from a previous chapter, colonization, is the takeover of land and people by a foreign group. Both colonization and slavery are fundamental historical events that curated the development of a darker-skinned global working class and a mostly White global dominating class. Racialized imperialism relies on the labor of low-income people of color located primarily in the Global South. One example is garment factories, which are one of the top industries in the world and are almost exclusively populated by poor Black and Brown women who are paid a fraction of the original wages negotiated by the brand and the contracted factory (Vemulakonda, 2021).

Modern-day neocolonial policies and practices have ensured that Europe and the United States (primarily) maintain control of land and the means of production in the Global South, in which labor is derived from marginalized racial groups. This kind of racial imperialism is necessary to maintain the historical dominance and perceived supremacy of Whiteness. As stated earlier in this chapter, dismantling racism requires a significant amount of work that ranges from shifts in cultural paradigms to the transformation of intricate social and political systems.

THE SUMMER UPRISINGS OF 2020

We will examine social movements in more detail in Chapter 12, but let's take a moment to reflect on the broadest movements of scope and scale in U.S. history, the landmark uprisings in the summer of 2020. The protests were ignited by the murder of George Floyd by Minneapolis, Minnesota, police on May 25, 2020. Amid the height of COVID-19, approximately 15–26 million people participated in protests across the United States. This protest movement was the largest in U.S. history (Buchanan, 2020). Although the protests have been classified as

"Black Lives Matter protests," many of the individuals involved were not affiliated with the global Black Lives Matter network or any particular, Black-led organization. The Brookings Institution (2022) analyzed data collected from a random sample of activists who participated in racial justice-focused protests in the summer of 2020 and here is what they found:

> As expected, we find that almost everyone who participated in these protests (94%) reported racial justice and/or police brutality/Black Lives Matter as one of their reasons for joining the crowds in the streets. In addition to these anti-racist motivations, protesters reported numerous other reasons for participating. About a-third of those surveyed also reported being motivated by women's rights (39%), LGBTQ rights (36%), or immigration rights (29%) to join the protests (para. 3).

The solidarity of individuals across various identities with the collective aim of opposing systemic racism, is also what makes this protest movement unique. Another distinctive aspect of this protest was the media, corporate, and governmental attention that was garnered. All of a sudden, corporations and governmental officials were proclaiming that "Black Lives Matter"! Unfortunately, this spectacular movement did not lead to significant changes within the system of policing, nor was it able to stop the unscrupulous murder of Black people at the hands of police.

Applying Sociology: Political Attitudes by Race and Ethnicity

Examine responses from the Pew Research Center (2021) survey on political attitudes by various demographic groups. Please address the following:

1. How might racial or ethnic identity shape one's political attitudes and choices?
2. What societal factors contribute to differences in political views among groups?

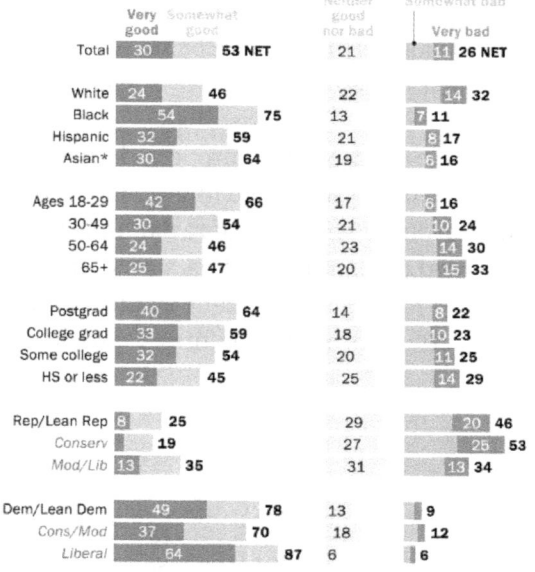

Image 7.2

SUMMARY: CONNECTING THE PIECES

In this chapter, we have examined how race and ethnicity are social constructions that have serious material implications in the real world. Although the idea that skin color would determine a person's intelligence, capabilities, or propensity to criminal behavior may seem ludicrous to some people today, these things were believed to be scientific facts in the not-so-distant past. Over time, with development of science and technology, as well as the progression of social attitudes, we now know that these ideas are absurd. However, their impact lingers. Racism is a social ill that impacts each and every member of a society. It is debilitating to the establishment of an optimal society. Even those who may not endure the harshest aspects of racialization share a world in which people around them are suffering, plighted, and plundered simply because they were born of a certain skin color. Poverty, crime, and sickness have direct links to race and ethnicity, and these are issues that plague entire societies. The silver lining is that race is a social construction. It is not impossible to deconstruct traditional racial systems. After all, they did not always exist! The task is an immense one though that will require the devotion of mass numbers of people and the transformation of cultural and social institutions.

REVIEW AND CRITICAL THINKING

Directions: Respond to the questions and prompts, based on what you have learned in this chapter:

1. Describe the social construction of race and ethnicity.
2. Discuss some of the myths about race that have been debunked over time.
3. How does racial and ethnic inequality impact your life?
4. How do conceptions of race vary over time and space?
5. Discuss racial and ethnic stratification in the culture and institutions of society.
6. What is racial imperialism? What structures and practices have constructed and maintained racial imperialism?
7. Describe the significance of the summer 2020 uprisings in terms of historical social movements aimed toward racial justice.
8. Why do you think it has been so difficult to undo or eliminate racism?

Credits
IMG 7.1: Source: https://mediadiversified.org/2014/01/23/ethnic-minority-no-global-majority/. Copyright © 2014 by Media Diversified.
IMG 7.2: Copyright © 2021 by Pew Research Center. Reprinted with permission.

■ CHAPTER 8

Families

Family is unique among other social institutions because of it is typically personal and intimate in nature. In other institutional arenas, such as the workplace or within governmental organizations, emotional expression and concern about sentimentality and personal needs are viewed less serious concerns

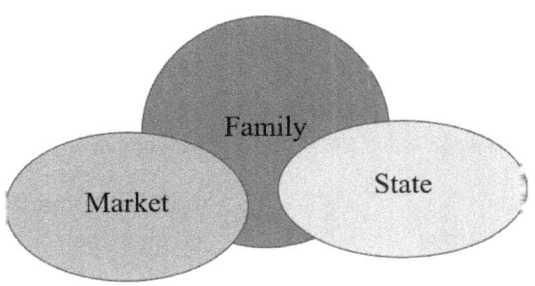

mage 8.1

than those of service and production. However, the micro-level concerns of the family should be a priority for the social institutions that shape, direct, and organize family life. Although individuals may personally define their families, the *state* imposes legal definitions that carry significant implications for accessibility and coverage. The *market* shapes family life through labor for economic pay, consumerism, and wealth accumulation. There are service and consumer markets built around family roles and practices. As an institution, families manifest in various social arenas, not simply physical spaces with clear parameters. For example, we know that there are homeless families in the United States who construct and carry out family life in transient outdoor spaces. Families contain positions that people occupy with guiding rules of interaction. Family roles serve to normalize ideas about power, authority, and the division of labor. Roles come with responsibilities, privileges, and in some cases disadvantages. Family overlaps and intertwines with the cultural, political, and economic institutions of the state. How these institutions define and depict family carries enormous weight in determining the conditions and sustainability of families.

✔ CHAPTER OBJECTIVES

After completing this chapter students should be able to do the following:

✔ **Contrast** various family structures and patterns in the United States.

✔ **Discuss** family as a social institution.

✔ **Provide** examples of international family laws and policies.

✔ **Explain** why it is difficult to adequately define families.

✔ **Summarize** the conflict perspective's view of family.

✔ **Recognize** the ways families are shaped by individuals and the state.

KEY TERMS

family   multigenerational household   social capital
nuclear family   life chances

WHAT MAKES A FAMILY?

Defining family can be difficult, and some may wonder why it is necessary at all. What are the outcomes or social implications of definitions of family? Does it really *matter* how we define family? The answer to the last question is a resounding yes! Elaborating on this will summarily address the first question as well. How family is defined can determine an employee's family health care benefits (many covering only married partners and their biological children), Social Security benefits (usually extended to spouses and dependents), and their options and rights related to inheritance. Unfortunately, it is in moments of health crises or death that this becomes most apparent to people.

We can generally define a **family** as a group of two or more people personally and/or legally bound by emotional, biological, or legal ties who care for one another and share activities. The U.S. Census Bureau is one of the leading organizations to provide demographic and economic information about United States since 1790. Many definitions and iterations of "family" have been used in the Census, but today's definition closely matches the one provided. An important qualification made in the U.S. Census definition of family is that a family *lives together in one household*. This criterion excludes personal and legal families that do not live in the same household. The Census Bureau's (2021a) "Estimates on America's

Families and Living Arrangements" reported that only 40% of all U.S. families lived with their own children. The same survey revealed that 14.6% of adults 18 years and older live alone. We can assume that some, if not most of these individuals, would personally claim to have a family or be a part of one.

However, subjective definitions of family are subordinate to prevailing social definitions. Institutional definitions of family are codified into law and thereby expand or limit people's options. Legal and therefore legitimized definitions of family are put forth by legislatures, agencies, and companies. We become aware of the parameters of the institutional arena of family as we engage in the labor force, consume within the market, and engage in the problems of general welfare and violence. This chapter's Applying Sociology exercise helps us to consider some of the other dynamics of personal and legal/institutional conceptions of family. Where do they intersect and diverge?

Applying Sociology: Defining Family: Personal and Legal Factors

Drawing from section 8.1 and reflecting on your own family type(s), fill in each square with information related to the nature and composition of each category.

Type of Family	Composition	Nature of Relationships	Residence	Values and Expectations	Provisions
Personal					
Legal					

FAMILIES IN THE UNITED STATES

Families in the United States have never been uniform. Prior to the Revolutionary War of 1776 that officiated "the United States," Indigenous populations traditionally lived in extended families that included parents, their children, grandparents, uncles, and aunts. Extended family networks made it unlikely that there would be orphans if children lost their parents (Coleman & Ganong, 2014). Early European settlers, strongly influenced by the Protestant religion doctrine, had nuclear families structured by conventional gender roles and authoritative parenting styles. They would have clash with later arrivals from Europe, like the Irish, who were Catholic, although they shared similar family structures. The enslaved who were forcibly brought from Africa and the Caribbean were prohibited from marriage and therefore formed informal kinship and caretaking networks.

Twenty-first-century American families are even more broad and diverse. In recent years there have been contestations about how what makes up a family and how families should be defined. According to the most recent U.S. Census (2022b) report on *Living Arrangements of Children*, the **nuclear family**, typically a married couple and their dependent children, constitutes 70.1% of the nation's families. Although this is a steep decline from the 1950s, it is still significant because it shows that these families have maintained through eras of transformative social, political, and economic changes.

As more adults choose to remain single and divorce is the outcome of nearly half of all marriages, single-parent households continue to grow. Another significant finding from the *Families and Living Arrangements* survey (U.S. Census Bureau, 2022a) revealed that the number of children living with their mother only has doubled. Single-family homes maintained by mothers now make up 80% of one-parent family groups. This, along with growing numbers of working mothers, runs in stark contrast to the father-/husband-led nuclear family of the American past.

Americans are also living much longer than they did in past centuries. An aging population necessitates social considerations around retirement and health care, but it also places significant strain on families that are responsible for the caregiving of elder members. This trend is reflected in the growing number of multigenerational families in the United States According to the Cohn et al. (2022), Census data from 1971–2021 show that the number of people living in multigenerational family households quadrupled. Multigenerational families now make up about 18% of the U.S. population. **Multigenerational households** typically include at least two generations of adults or grandparents and grandchildren. There are both personal and social benefits to multigenerational homes. Americans living in multigenerational households are less likely to be low income than those living in other types of households. Members of these families also report caregiving as a primary reason for their living arrangement.

Asian, Hispanic, and Black American populations are more likely than White Americans to live with extended family, especially if they are immigrants. It is predicted that by 2050, White Americans will make up only half of the total U.S. population as Latino, Asian, and Black populations are projected to triple in size (Benokraitis, 2015). If these predictions play out, we can expect the number of mutigenerational households to continue to grow.

THE REPRODUCTION OF ADVANTAGE AND DISADVANTAGE IN FAMILIES

Max Weber (1864–1920), a pioneering 20th-century German sociologist, contributed the sociological concept of **life chances** to describe one's opportunity to achieve various personal and material life outcomes. Weber was concerned with the *practical* ability of people to achieve their life goals, taking into consideration external forces such as one's economic position and level of prestige within society. The "American dream" of owning a home one day is idealistic, but the practical chances of doing so are limited to those who can afford it.

The income of parents or caretakers in a home directly impacts the life chances of children and dependents. The **social capital**, or resources that one has by virtue of relationships and connections within a social network, can be determining factors in whether one will know how to read before kindergarten and one's likelihood of completing college. Social capital is something that rich and low-income families can have, but the amount of literal money held by these families separates them into distinct classes.

Generational Wealth

In many of America's upper-class families, significant amounts of wealth are passed from generation to generation. However, it is not only wealth that is passed along, but social connections, lifestyle, education, and property. A particular class consciousness is developed among the wealthy as they share common experiences, interests, and exclusive access and memberships that are inaccessible to the poor (Cohen, 2021). The social and material capital of these families can extend to multiple generations and sets them apart as a small elite group with the United States.

Generational Poverty

Contrary to the "rags-to-riches" stories that permeate American media, only about 8% of children raised in the bottom 20% of the income distribution are able to climb to the top 20% as adults, according to the article *The 'American Dream' of Upward Mobility Is Broken. Look at the Numbers* (Rank & Eppard, 2021). The authors of the article, professors Rank and Eppard write that:

> Equality of opportunity is also much less viable in the US than in other OECD (Organization for Economic Co-operation and Development) countries. American life expectancy varies by up to 20 years depending on the zip code of residence. Quality of education also differs widely depending on the wealth of the neighborhood that families reside in. And the chances of being victimized by a crime, exposed to environmental toxins or having unmet healthcare needs is far greater for America's poor than those impoverished in all other OECD countries. (para. 6)

Drawing from the information we have covered so far; we can ascertain that social class is a mediating variable of family life. Structural factors such as the economy, technology, family policies, and cultural ideologies produce either opportunities or constraints for families. Social capital alone cannot provide the necessary resources for poor individuals to improve their life chances. Therefore, efforts to better sustain American families must address the factors that impact their material conditions.

"THE WORLD'S MOST PROGRESSIVE FAMILY CODE": A LOOK AT CUBA'S NEW FAMILY CODE

After 3.5 years of direct consultations with citizens, over 79,000 meetings held throughout the country, and 25 revisions, the Cuban government passed a historic referendum on its new family code. Prior to the September 25, 2022, referendum, only constitutional referendums had been held in the country. Cuba is now the first country in the world to have submitted a family code to popular consultation and referendum. Cubans were decisive in their support of the referendum, with 66.87% of respondents voting yes (People's Dispatch, 2022).

The new family code is said to be one of the most progressive, inclusive, and revolutionary in the world. The new code legalizes equal adoption rights regardless of sexual orientation, provides a guaranteed income for caregivers, rights for people with disabilities, legalizes equal marriage, promotes the equal distribution of domestic responsibilities among men and women, recognizes the role of grandparents in the family, provides resources for family mediation, recognizes the rights of surrogate mothers, and outlaws child marriage and corporal punishment, to name a few of its features. The code also offers more support for institutions that assist families and will monitor its enforcement monthly as new penal codes are created to ensure the recognition of the law and its enforcement across social spheres (People's Dispatch, 2022).

How was Cuba able to pass such a referendum? Why aren't there more like these in the world? These are questions for us to reflect on and not necessarily answer here, but I will offer a few responses. Cuba is an island of about 11 million people, geographically isolated by the surrounding Atlantic Ocean and Caribbean Sea. Cuba has also endured a U.S. trade blockade for the last 60 years. The blockade was enacted just after the success of the Cuban Revolution in 1959, which resulted in the development of a socialist society. These social conditions are important to acknowledge in order to understand the nature of Cuban life and Cuban people. Cuban society is built around mutual care, trust, and goodwill. A socialist economic structure means that industry is nationalized and that the basic necessities of life, such as health care, housing, and education, are ensured by the government. Politically, this referendum is Cuba's ultimate exercise in direct democracy. Cuba was able to successfully pass such as broad and transformative referendum because Cuba is a people-centered society. The consumer market does not set the standards for social life, nor does an elite government. The people or human-centered approach taken toward social life and social arrangements in Cuba inevitably bestows high regard for the lives of all inhabitants, young or old, gay or straight, able or disabled. The fact that Cuba is still living its socialist revolution and is very proud of it also speaks to the mind-set of the Cuban people regarding their value of equality and justice. These things are reflected in the monumental and illustrious family code that has been enacted in the country.

THE FUTURE OF THE FAMILY

It is difficult to predict what lies ahead for families in the United States, but we can get a sense of what some members of the society are most concerned about from national survey data. The Pew Research Center (2019) survey of U.S. adults revealed that many people are apprehensive about the economic circumstances of families by 2050. The group with most trepidation were White men between the ages of 50 and 64. Black men

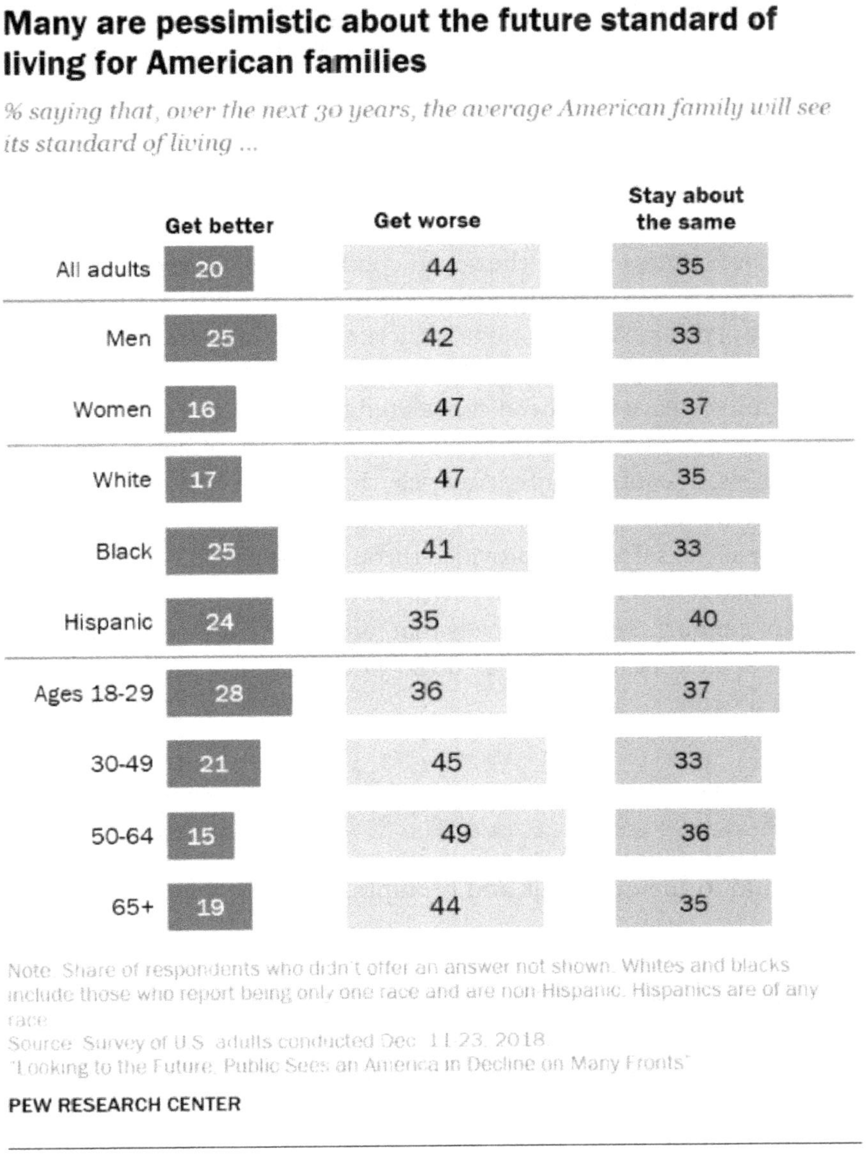

Many are pessimistic about the future standard of living for American families

% saying that, over the next 30 years, the average American family will see its standard of living ...

	Get better	Get worse	Stay about the same
All adults	20	44	35
Men	25	42	33
Women	16	47	37
White	17	47	35
Black	25	41	33
Hispanic	24	35	40
Ages 18-29	28	36	37
30-49	21	45	33
50-64	15	49	36
65+	19	44	35

Note: Share of respondents who didn't offer an answer not shown. Whites and blacks include those who report being only one race and are non-Hispanic. Hispanics are of any race.
Source: Survey of U.S. adults conducted Dec. 11-23, 2018.
"Looking to the Future, Public Sees an America in Decline on Many Fronts"

PEW RESEARCH CENTER

Image 8.2

ages 18–29 are most optimistic about the future standard of living for U.S. families. As previously noted, the social capital that can be generated through kinship and caretaking networks are limited by one's economic capacity. Family life is no longer isolated within small communities; it is an institution that is dependent on other institutions to assist in the personal and social development of individuals throughout the life course. This transformation in family life has created a reliance on the market that provides labor to pay and goods for economic exchange, which reinforces the need to accumulate wealth to survive. Such far-reaching changes in family life call for a reconfiguring of the state's relationship to families as well. Although labeled "socialist," things like free health care, free or reduced college education, and housing-first policies would provide families with the support that they need and eliminate the ongoing economic concerns that lead to the demise of so many U.S. families.

SUMMARY: CONNECTING THE PIECES

Families in the United States reflect the social conditions within society. At worst, they demonstrate the material outcomes of various kinds of inequality. In their best light, they represent a rainbow of diverse compositions, structures, and practices. Like the world itself, families will continue to ebb and flow with the social, political, and economic changes of social systems. Families have long been considered the foundation of societies, although many of these notions are wrapped up in historical ideas about gender roles and reproduction. Nevertheless, in contemporary America, the family is one of the most important institutions because no other provides free, long-term care, support, and intimacy. There are fewer and fewer social safety nets provided through government services, and the daily grind of life in a production-centered society will likely continue to fuel a yearning for closeness and havens of comfort. These are needs that families are uniquely equipped to fulfill. However, they are at their best capacity to do so when there is a structural investment in their collective well-being.

REVIEW AND CRITICAL THINKING

Directions: Respond to the questions and prompts, based on what you have learned in this chapter:

1. Why are governmental definitions of family significant? Why should we care about how families are defined?
2. Differentiate between personal and legal families and provide examples of each.
3. Discuss the role of the state and the market in family life.
4. Provide an overview of the current state of U.S. families. Discuss their compositions, strengths, and challenges.

5. How do families reproduce advantages and disadvantages? What is the role of social capital in the reproduction of inequality?
6. Why is it important to codify the rights and provisions of families into law?
7. Compare and contrast the Cuban family code with other family codes around the world.
8. In what ways will the social, political, and economic changes of the future impact families?

Credit
IMG 8.2: Copyright © 2018 by Pew Research Center. Reprinted with permission.

CHAPTER 9

Health Care and Aging

SOCIAL DETERMINANTS OF HEALTH

Social determinants of health are the nonmedical factors that shape health outcomes. These include many variables housed within the categories in the figure, such as socioeconomic status, access to health care, and social stigma. Social constructionists sometimes encounter the predicament of determining if the "chicken" or "egg" came first in these types of analyses. One could argue, and with the support of some credible sources, that medical factors and conditions can also be socially determined. For example, birth defects can be genetic, but genetic conditions are also shaped by the social environment and social position of a mother before and during pregnancy. Birth defects, in some

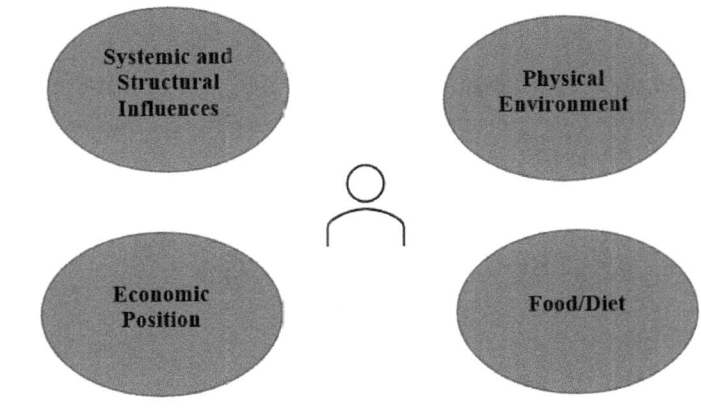

Image 9.1

cases, are directly attributed to infection or drug exposure (Centers for Disease Control and Prevention [CDC], 2022). Using the social constructionist framework, the social determinants of health will be emphasized in this chapter.

We will first explore the health care system as a social institution within the social structure of the United States. We will look at the functions and components of the institution, as well as how it is informed and shaped by other institutions. As we examine health care systems around the world and contemplate the experience of aging in different places, we will consider the social *implications* of health. Together, we will look at how health contributes to the overall well-being of a person, their physical and mental health. A review of reforms and transformations within the U.S. health care system will provide a historical context that can be used as a basis for a contemporary understanding of the institution today and the health outcomes of the population.

✔ CHAPTER OBJECTIVES

After completing this chapter students should be able to do the following:

✔ **Describe** health care as a social institution.

✔ **Differentiate** between different types of health care systems.

✔ **Analyze** the history of health care reform in the United States.

✔ **Summarize** the social construction of aging.

✔ **Explain** trends and experiences in aging in the United States.

✔ **Discuss** how ageism is socially constructed and variable by social group.

KEY TERMS

social determinants	health care	ageism
health	emergent social institution	generational framing

HEALTH CARE AS A SOCIAL INSTITUTION

Health can be defined as a condition typically measured by three components: physical, mental, and social. **Health care** is any activity that improves one's health and well-being. Keep in mind that definitions of health and health care are cultural and can vary from place to place and group to group. In sociology, health care is an **emergent social institution**, a social entity developed over time along with societal changes and transformations, organized to meet one or more of society's basic needs. While humans have always needed some form of health care, the intricate institution that we are familiar with today is a product of modernity. Today, there are over 6,000 hospitals and nearly 3,000 medical clinics in the United States. The health care industry employs about 22 million people, making up 14% of all U.S. workers (Laughlin, Anderson, Martinez, & Gayfield, 2021).

Social institutions not only carry out some of the vital work of society, but they transmit and reinforce cultural values and norms that ultimately shape and guide behavior. An analysis of social institutions informs us of social functions and dysfunctions and the intersections of institutions and groups of people. For example, in this chapter we will discuss how health care is shaped by the political and economic institutions of a society. We will also review some of the cultural implications of health care, such as how ideas about health and illness shape how we determine sickness and the ways we address it. Functionalist theorists would argue that societies should make wellness a priority because sick people cannot perform the roles needed to keep society operating properly. They may do this on the macro level by establishing health facilities such as clinics and hospitals. On the micro level societies may adopt certain cultural understandings such as what sickness looks, feels, or even smells like. In the United States, health care is also an arena of competition for scarce resources since it is largely a for-profit service. However, throughout U.S. history there have been various alternatives proposed but never adopted.

U.S. HEALTH CARE REFORM: A TIMELINE

In order to understand the U.S. health care system, one has to first recognize that it is a for-profit institution. This means that most occupants of the United States must pay for medical care. Coverage can come in the form of employer-based coverage (includes premium payments), government health insurance (low, but not always completely free), and other types of private health insurance (paid by holder). There are some groups that *qualify* for free or low-cost health care, such as older people and children (Medicaid and Children's Health Insurance Program), but there are specific criteria for granting these provisions. Currently about 76.4 million individuals in the United States are enrolled in Medicaid and the CHIP (United Healthcare Community Plan, 2021). According to the Kaiser Family Foundation (2022), there are 27.5 million people who are currently without health insurance in the United States. Since states have the authority to determine some aspects of governmental funding for health care, public coverage varies by state. The Kaiser report on the uninsured in the United States notes that "most uninsured people are in low-income families and have at least one worker in the family ... People of color are generally at higher risk of being uninsured than White people, though Asian people have the lowest uninsured rate ' (para. 4). Therefore, health care insurance is another distinct class division in the United States, a vital resource that is most accessible to those with personal money or jobs that cover some portion of their coverage. With health care costs increasing every decade since 1980 and the United States charging more for basic services such as doctor's visits and conventional birth deliveries than many other high-income countries (Benokraitis, 2014), we can expect this trend to continue unless there is a fundamental transformation of the system itself. There have been various points throughout U.S. history in which broader coverage or even free national health care has been proposed. However, most of these plans were not successfully implemented. Those that are currently in operation are in bold.

Here is a historical timeline of proposed legislation for reform or transformation of U.S. health care (Gore, 2013; Giddens et. al., 2015; Gore, 2013; Hoffman, 2003).

- **1915**: The American Association for Labor Legislations proposes *compulsory health insurance* that would "protect workers against both wage loss and medical costs during sickness" (2003, para. 5).
- **1925**: The Committee on the Cost of Medical Care (CCMC) was established to address the rising cost of physician and hospital care. The CCMC and its staff issued 15 separate reports over 5 years, with the most controversial recommendation being for national health insurance, either voluntary or compulsory through taxation.
- **1935**: The **Social Security Act** is passed in which U.S. Social Security "insurance" was supported through contributions in the form of taxes on individuals' wages and employers' payrolls rather than directly from government funds. Comprehensive national health programs were excluded from the final bill.
- **1943**: Wagner-Murray-Dingell Bill (named after Congressional sponsors) is drafted that proposed a national medical insurance program financed through social security payroll taxes.
- **1965**: **Medicare**, medical coverage of the elderly, is added to the Social Security Act.
- **1993**: The Health Security Bill is introduced by the Clinton administration proposed a complex system of 'health alliances' that would preserve both employer-based coverage and the commercial insurance industry" (2003, para. 20).
- **2010**: The Obama administration implements the **Affordable Care Act**. The law consists of three primary goals:
  - Make affordable health insurance available to more people. The law provides consumers with subsidies ("premium tax credits") that lower costs for households with incomes between 100% and 400% of the federal poverty level (FPL).
    - If your income is above 400% FPL, you may still qualify for a premium tax credit.
    - If your income is at or below 150% FPL, you may qualify to enroll in or change marketplace coverage through a special enrollment period.
  - Expand the Medicaid program to cover all adults with income below 138% of the FPL (not implemented by all states).
  - Support innovative medical care delivery methods designed to lower the costs of health care generally.

A LOOK AT 3 HEALTH CARE SYSTEMS

Health care systems vary around the globe. The geographic, political, and economic dimensions of a society largely determine the type of health care system that is implemented. For some countries, health care is a human right, something that is free and accessible to the entire population. In other countries, health care is a social service that comes at varying costs. In this section we will briefly examine some of the key features of health care systems in three different countries around the world. It is often difficult to obtain accurate and up-to-date information on health care due to lack of public reporting in some cases or outdated information in others. For this reason, several sources were reviewed to compose these summaries. However, things are constantly in flux in the world that we live in, and much variation exists across regions and cultural groups, even within the same country.

Health Care in China

Medical insurance in China consists of two parts: (a) a unified account managed by authorities to cover expenses for hospitalization in the case of major diseases, and (b) a personal spending account for the outpatient treatment of more common diseases. Over 1.3 billion of the 1.4 billion people who live in China are covered by medical insurance. However, there are some limitations to coverage. When one's personal account cannot cover costs, people have to pay out-of-pocket for common illnesses. Furthermore, public health insurance usually does not cover many out-patient services like the purchase of medicines and medical examinations (China Global Television Network [CGTN], 2023a). While China's large aging population, in addition to limited medical resources, produces challenges for the country, China is reforming their health care insurance system to improve the use of medical funds and help most vulnerable populations. Additionally, China is developing smart technologies such as artificial intelligence to match patients more precisely to doctors and build medical technologies that can provide diagnoses, treatment, and follow-up services. According to Medical AI product director, Zhao Jing, "The Medical AI products mainly rely on medical artificial intelligence and natural language processing technologies developed by Tencent and simulate the growth and learning process of a human doctor by studying medical literature, clinical guidelines, clinical records and other data" (CGTN, 2023b, para. 7).

Health Care in Egypt

In Egypt, the Health Insurance Organization (HIO) provides all Egyptians with health coverage and care. The four basic classes of beneficiaries under HIO are all employees working in the government sector, some public and private sector employees, pensioners, and widows. The public health system in Egypt has its challenges. Only about 60% of the population is covered by the HIO as citizens do have the ability to opt out of the compulsory insurance provided by formal sector employment. Issues such as underfunding, low-quality care, lack of medical equipment, and qualified personnel many Egyptians seek care from private facilities (Fasseeh et al., 2022). However, in 2018 the Universal Health Insurance Law was put into place with the intention of restructuring the system by providing coverage to all and making health services affordable for citizens. In 2020 the World Bank provided $400 million in support of Egypt's Universal Health Insurance System. The full implementation of universal health insurance should help to decrease health expenditures for citizens in which 60% of health care spending is paid out-of-pocket for all types of care (World Bank, 2020).

Health Care in Cuba

In Cuba, medical care is considered a human right and is written into the constitution. Free health care is guaranteed to all Cubans, and there are no private hospitals in the country. The Laboratorios Farmacéuticos Oriente is one major part of the country's exceptional medical system. It is from this laboratory that Cuba has developed five landmark COVID-19 vaccines in various stages. Cuba was the first country in the world to develop a vaccine for children from 3–11 years old. Cuban doctors and nurses report that they were encouraged by late president Fidel Castro to development a biotech pharmaceutical industry that scientifically trained doctors and researchers. Cuba produces many of its own medical supplies and is developing natural and holistic products to treat ailments on an ongoing basis (Arenstein & Neeley, 2023). They can do this, even under an economic blockade, because of the country's investment in collective health care and the rigorous training of doctors in not only contemporary medicine, but holistic and Indigenous medicines as well. I had a direct encounter with the Cuban medical system when I became sick while visiting the country. Although I was only suffering from a migraine headache, I was consulted for over an hour by both a doctor and a nurse. I was given natural remedies such as lemon juice and a vitamin C injection, and within 30 minutes I had fully recovered. Those same medical professionals came to check on me twice more that day and even the next morning. When I asked how much I should pay for their services, they were surprised and responded that there would be no fee for my care.

Applying Sociology: Which Place Would I Rather Grow Old?

Drawing from Section 9.3 (and your own research), place a checkmark in the box if the provision is present in that country. After you have selected the provisions, please answer the question that follows.

Place/Country	Free Medicines	Low or Affordable Health Insurance (Paid by Insured)	Free Doctor Exams	Free Universal Coverage
Hungary, Europe				
Egypt, Africa				
China, Asia				
Cuba/Latin America/ Caribbean				

1. Which country would you prefer to grow old in? Why?

_____

_____

_____

_____

_____

_____

THE SOCIAL IMPLICATIONS OF AGE IN POPULATION DYNAMICS

Like other demographic variables, understanding the distribution of age across a population is significant to social analysis. It informs what we know about fertility and mortality rates, reveals which age categories are dominant or less populous, and brings forth considerations about social services and public accommodations required to meet the needs of these groups. However, age is a social construction. Certainly, humans and all living things will get "older" as they keep living, but the way calendar years are counted, and the social meanings attached to specific ages are determined by people and are cultural variants. Getting "old" in the United States could mean reaching the age of 60 or beyond. However, living beyond the age of 60 could be viewed as exceptional in a country like Afghanistan where the median age is 18 years, and the average life expectancy is 64 years (International Labor Organization, 2019). Chronological age is most socially significant in the United States because it provides a sort of "rites of passage" into various experiences throughout the life course. For example, a person can get a driver's license at the age of 16, join the army at 18 years, legally drink alcohol at 21 years, rent vehicles at age 25, and become eligible for retirement benefits at age 62. From U.S. population polls and surveys that are consistently conducted by numerous organizations, such as the U.S. Census Bureau and the Pew Research Center, we can ascertain that younger people tend to be more politically progressive (not necessarily socially) and more deviant than older groups of people. Obviously, younger people have different primary needs than the elderly, in things such as access and opportunities for education and employment. Societies with significant populations of people over the age of 65 may give more attention to the health care and retirement systems. As an illustration, at the time of this writing France is enduring massive protests as over 1 million people have taken to the streets to challenge the passing of a French Parliament decision to increase the retirement age from 62 to 64 years without a public vote. The reason given for the pension reform according to French president Emmanuel Macron was "to erase deficits in the system by 2030" (Aljazeera, 2023). Countries, particularly those in the Global South, with predominantly young populations (under the age of 30), such as Burkina Faso, may be more likely to experience uprisings and revolts in response to local and/or international governmental measures. The Arab Spring that catapulted political activity in several countries throughout the Middle East and Northern Africa in 2011 consisted mostly of students and young people (Robinson & Merrow, 2020). A balanced distribution of ages across a population would be ideal in most cases, but due to the diversity of societies and their various social, political, and economic terrains, this is unlikely to occur.

THE SOCIAL CONSTRUCTION OF AGEISM

The ironic thing about **ageism**, systematic prejudice or discrimination based on one's age, is that most people in the United States not only want to live long lives, but also just want to *live* (MDVIP, 2022). The biological aging process inevitably moves every living person or thing toward death, but death has not always been something associated with *old* age. In earlier years of U.S. history, death was more common across age groups and typical among infants less than 1 year of age (Ferrante, 2015). All the same, one aspect of the social construction of age are perceptions about one's social value, ability, and capacity at different stages in the life course. Other social signifiers of age, such as gray hair, wrinkles, smooth and clear skin, a full head of hair, and so on, intersect with cultural beauty standards to differentially situate individuals in relation to social prestige and material resources. However, we must come back to what we know about the Western world's influence on dominant narratives and values around the globe. It can be argued that ageism itself is a Western construct. Scholars of African history and tradition, such as Oyèrónkẹ́ Oyěwùmí and Cheikh Anta Diop, have argued that age is a primary element of social status in traditional African societies. They note that age is a primary organizing principle in many African societies, especially those that still have traditional practices. In societies such as these, age is revered and rights, authority, and independence are conferred by age. In the United States we see that ethnic groups like Asian, Latino, and Black people tend to live in multigenerational homes at much higher rates than White Americans. These living arrangements indicate ideas and values related to both family and age.

Unlike other "isms," ageism is one that is widespread but often goes unchallenged. It is embedded into U.S. culture and institutions through the use of ridicule, jokes, and stereotypes about older people. Societal shifts due to the progression of capitalism and capitalist development have also played a role in the social devaluation of older people. It is assumed that they are not as physically mobile and agile as most youth; therefore, their ability to do certain types of work and for how long is limited. Industrialization, mechanization, and digitization has increased the value of technical skills more so than that of lived experiences. Keeping up with the latest changes in technology can be a challenge for older people, but this is not exclusive to this age group. Ageism relies on assumptions and stereotypes that are reinforced through culture as well as our social interactions. Most people socialize in age-segregated groups and environments (i.e., schools, community groups, neighborhoods, clubs), which prevent the possibility of dispelling misconceptions about people of different ages. Anti-ageism advocate Ashton Applewhite (2021) argues in her essay "Let's Climb Out of the Generation Trap" that **generational framing**, which is the classification of birth or age groups into cohorts, sanctions and supports age segregation, fosters age stereotypes and generalizations, validates the notion of "intergenerational conflict," and undermines equity, solidarity, and collective action needed for social good. Ultimately, ageism serves to further divide individuals politically and economically in ways that are mostly invisible but conducive to maintaining a social hierarchy of power and privilege.

SUMMARY: CONNECTING THE PIECES

Throughout this chapter we have discussed health care in the United States and internationally, as well as some of the social considerations and implications of age. Although the chapter has examined health predominantly from a systemic perspective, we acknowledge the role of culture in constructing, distributing, and reinforcing notions about governmental health care provisions, what it means to be sick, and how illness should be handled. Media and culture also heavily shape our ideas, beliefs, and values related to age. Although there is not a perfect linear relationship between old age and poor health, this correlation occupies the minds of many individuals. It seems that many people in the United States want to live long lives but hold stigma and fear about death. These sentiments are often turned into prejudices and discrimination toward those who are older in age or even *appear* older. Like other aspects of identity that hold social significance, age is a variable of difference. But all too often difference is socially constructed to produce unequal outcomes in treatment and access to opportunities and resources. Children and youth who are dependents are beholden to the health care coverage or insurance of their parents or guardians. Adults who live in countries without universal health coverage may receive some health insurance from their employers but may not be covered after retirement. These outcomes produce real and consequential advantages and disadvantages for individuals and groups. We will further concretize the relationship between culture and systems in the last few chapters of the textbook as we examine the social institutions that frame and shape our lives.

REVIEW AND CRITICAL THINKING

Directions: Respond to the questions and prompts, based on what you have learned in this chapter:

1. As a social institution, what is the social role and function of health care?
2. What are some ways in which the health care institution is shaped by and intersected with other social institutions?
3. Name and describe two transformative health care policies that have been proposed or implemented in the United States?
4. Discuss features of at least one health care system outside of the United States.
5. Why is age a significant variable of analysis for studying human populations?
6. What is ageism? Provide an example. Are there other meanings of aging and old age other than something that is problematic or diminutive?

■ **CHAPTER 10**

Geopolitical Economy

THE *UNMIGHTY* DOLLAR?

At least since the mid-2000s, there has been public concern about the use and value of the American dollar globally. Joseph Quinlan, managing director and chief market strategist at U.S. Trust, Bank of America Private Wealth Management, wrote in 2004 that "the sinking dollar could be a sign that the world is no longer willing to underwrite the designs of U.S. foreign policy. To a large degree, a rebound in

Image 10.1

the U.S. dollar could hinge on a revamped U.S. foreign policy" (Quinlan, 2004, para. XX). He goes further to state, "The dollar's swoon has been blamed on America's debtor status, manifested in a current account deficit approaching 6% of GDP and a federal budget deficit of well over $400 billion—greater than the output of most nations" (Quinlan, 2004, para. 7). During Donald Trump's presidency (2016–2020), U.S. debt reached more than $25 trillion due the Treasury Department's issuance of $20 billion in 20-year bonds (Ahmed, 2020). The 2008 banking crisis in the United States, followed by the March 2023 collapse of Silvergate Bank, Silicon Valley Bank, and Signature Bank, has reduced global confidence in the dollar.

For decades, the U.S. dollar has been the principal reserve currency for global transactions. According to the Congressional Research Service (2022), "About half of international trade is invoiced in dollars, and about half of all international loans and global debt securities are denominated in dollars. In foreign exchange markets, where currencies are traded, dollars are involved in nearly 90% of all transactions" (para. 2). When it comes to the **petrodollar**, U.S. dollars used to pay for gas and oil from exporting countries, about 80% of these transactions are completed in U.S. dollars. However, amid the Ukraine–Russia war that began in February of 2022, which is heavily fueled by U.S. and NATO aid (about $100 billion given to Ukraine in aid at the time of this writing), economic sanctions on Russia have led to several countries deciding to use local currencies for their transactions in case they too are sanctioned by the United States. Russia led this movement by requiring that countries who buy oil from them pay in rubles, Russia's currency. With Russia being the second largest oil producer in the world, this is not insignificant. Many countries in what is referred to as the Global South and East have depended on oil from Russia, as well as many countries in Europe such as Germany, Poland, and Greece. The irony of U.S. economic sanctions on Russia is that it has increased the value of the ruble. Saudi Arabia, the world's third largest oil producer, confirmed in January of 2023 that they were considering selling oil in other currencies. Around the same time, China's president Xi Jinping announced that China would be buying oil and gas from the Persian Gulf region with its own currency, the renminbi, instead of dollars. The escalation away from the U.S. dollar has not stopped there, South Africa's Foreign Minister Naledi Pandor stated that BRICS, which is a collective of some of the world's emerging economies of Brazil, Russia, India, China, and South Africa, is currently planning to "develop a fairer system of monetary exchange" to weaken the "dominance of the dollar" (Norton, 2023, para. 7). BRICS nations plan to do this by developing a joint currency that would eliminate their reliance on U.S. and Western currencies. It appears that a global campaign of de-dollarization is underway, and what is emerging is a multipolar currency world, one in which multiple currencies are used in global trade and finance and no singular currency is dominant.

✔ CHAPTER OBJECTIVES

After completing this chapter students should be able to do the following:

✔ **Define** *hegemony* and provide at least two examples to illustrate its presence in the world.

✔ **Compare and contrast** major political systems around the world.

✔ **Describe** how the center/source of power differs among various political systems.

✔ **Discuss** the key characteristics of capitalist, socialist, and mixed economies.

✔ **Explain** both differing ideas about development and the types of development present in one or more country.

✔ **Define** *multipolarity* and provide at least two examples of its presence in the world.

KEY TERMS

geopolitics	totalitarian	plutocracy
petrodollar	democracy	democratic socialism
hegemony	representative democracy	communism
authority	superdelegates	capitalism
politics	voter disenfranchisement	socialism
authoritarian	voter apathy	multipolarity

MAJOR POLITICAL SYSTEMS OF THE WORLD

Geopolitics can be defined as international relations that are shaped by political and geographical factors. Over the last several decades, the world has become more deeply integrated and interdependent. This is primarily due to global finance organizations like the International Monetary Fund and the World Bank, which have orchestrated financial agreements (and a pattern of dependency through debt), along with increases in intercontinental trade and the consistent migration of people, both voluntarily and involuntarily. Geography is an important factor in our understanding of national and global politics. In this chapter **politics** will be discussed in two ways: first as a social institution in which people acquire power through the exercise of democratic rights and one in which people acquire power through elected or selected positions of influence and governance; second, as the personal and/or socially attributed aspects of one's identity that are deterministic of their social position and agency (or power) in the society. Although there are various political systems that could be explored, we will focus on two systems that appear to be polar opposites—authoritarian and democratic political systems.

Authoritarian Political Systems

We will begin this section by defining *authoritarianism*. Authoritarianism is not only a type of political system, but also a type of social control and dominance that operates on the micro levels of societies. In the specific context of this chapter, **authoritarianism** can be defined as a political system governed by a particular person or family with limited or no popular participation in government. There is not a consensus on specific countries that have authoritarian governments, but a few that have received the label include Italy under Benito Mussolini (1922–43), the Soviet Union under Joseph Stalin (1924–53), and Nazi Germany under Adolf Hitler (1933–45). These are countries that have also been called **totalitarian**, a political system in which the state regulates all aspects of people's public and private lives.

Since the end of World War II, many, if not all, countries that have received the label of authoritarian or totalitarian have been non-Western hemisphere countries and/or countries that do not have capitalist economic systems. For example, China, Cuba, and Libya (under the leadership of Muammar Gaddafi) are often referred to as countries led (or previously led) by dictators that suppress the rights and freedoms of their inhabitants. However, national surveys and personal statements from the citizens of these countries show otherwise. On a survey of Chinese public opinion over time, which includes a decade-long survey of more than 31,000 Chinese citizens from 2003 to 2016, it was concluded that "Chinese citizen satisfaction with government has increased virtually across the board" (Cunningham et al., 2020, p. 4). The study found a nearly universal rise in the average satisfaction toward all four levels of the Chinese government—township, county, province, and central government levels. This study is unique in that it is the longest academic study of Chinese public opinion ever conducted by a research institution based outside of China (Dzodin, 2020).

Cuba regularly has massive voter turnout and citizen contribution in national elections and legislation development. An example of this has been covered in a previous chapter with the examination of Cuba's family code passed in September of 2022, in which 74% of Cubans took part in the vote and 66.87% of respondents voted affirmatively (Neeley, 2023). In March of 2023, Cuban voters elected 470 legislators for the country's National Assembly. Voter turnout was even larger for this election, with 76% of Cubans placing a vote (Meneses, 2023). It is extremely rare in the United States for even 50% of voting-eligible people to turnout to vote in national elections (Desilver, 2022).

When it comes to Libya it is important to note that the people of Libya did not overturn their government; it was the foreign intervention of NATO in 2011 that resulted in the murder of Muammar Gaddafi and an ensuing state of civil war and economic and social deterioration that has occurred ever since. Although criticisms can be made toward any leader, and Gaddafi is no exception, the standard of living for Libyans increased significantly when Gaddafi was in leadership (Ruehl, 2022).

One of the most significant aspects of developing a sociological consciousness is a critical examination of the ideas that we hold, where they come from, and alternative perspectives that may differ from our own. It is important for us to examine media from a variety of sources, including those outside of the United States. Some characteristics of totalitarianism include the use of propaganda to control people's actions, a specific political ideology, and a single ruling group or party of elites. As we will learn in the next section, countries with democratic political systems are not necessarily exempt of these characteristics. Just as all economic systems have mixed economic types, political systems are also assorted.

Democratic Political Systems

Before we examine democratic political systems, lets first establish a definition of democracy. A **democracy** can be defined as a political system in which the government is accountable to citizens and power is yielded by the masses through elected representatives. Other components of an ideal-type democracy include the guarantee of civil liberties, constitutional limits placed on governmental powers, government structure and processes clear to the public, and written documents such as constitutions or bills of rights as the basis of legal systems (Ballantine & Roberts, 2012). According to the Pew Research Center (2019), more than half of the world's countries are democracies. The United States is said to have a **representative democracy**, one in which citizens elect representatives to serve as bridges between themselves and the government. Democratic political systems have at least two political parties that compete in elections to secure local or national positions. The U.S. Constitution requires that each state have two senators and a minimum of one member in the House of Representatives. However, there are some exceptions. Territories under U.S. jurisdiction such as Guam and Puerto Rico have *nonvoting* delegates in the U.S. Congress, and citizens of those territories cannot vote in U.S. elections. Additionally, Washington, DC, which is not a state, gets three electoral votes in the Electoral College, which ultimately decides who will be elected president and vice president in the United States. Each state has a set number of electors or votes in the Electoral College. The number of electors is determined by the population of the state. Many are critical of the "winner-takes-all" framework in which the electee with more than 50% of the vote get the position. This does not reflect **proportional representation** in which each party is given a number of seats that correspond with the percentage of votes received in the election. Instead, the popular vote of the masses can be eschewed by the electoral votes of the most populous states, which have more votes in the Electoral College. The most recent examples of this are the 2000 presidential election between Al Gore and George W. Bush and the 2016 presidential election between Donald Trump and Hillary Clinton. Both Al Gore and Hillary Clinton received more of the popular vote but lost the Electoral College vote and therefore lost the presidency. Furthermore, many have argued that the establishment of the Supreme Court is undemocratic, in that members are not elected by the public and hold their positions for life. **Superdelegates**, which were implemented in 1984 and are unique to the Democratic Party, are unelected delegates who are free to support any candidate for the presidential nomination at the Democratic National Convention. They were implemented in an attempt to prevent the elimination of future candidates considered by elite members of government to be unelectable. Superdelegates, which now make up about 20% of all delegates, are intended to act as a check on ideologically extreme or inexperienced candidates. However, superdelegates are not obligated to support the candidate of their constituents' choice, therefore undermining the purpose of a representative democracy (Unger, 2008). Ironically, **direct democracies** in which citizens make major policy decisions and work in communities to govern their social life and develop mutual civic trust are more common in countries often labeled authoritarian, such as Cuba and Vietnam.

POLITICAL PARTIES AND ELECTIONS

Ideally, in a representative democracy elected representatives support and convey the interests and concerns of those they represent. In response, the government is supposed to be amenable to the people. This is an ideal type of democracy in which many fall short of these aspirations. The two-party voting system in the United States is unique among other economically affluent nations such as Germany, France, and Canada, for instance, that have multiparty political system. In fact, multiparty political systems are the most common throughout the world. There are certainly critiques and challenges with multiparty democratic systems, one being the difficulties that can arise in forming strong coalitions due to dissimilar ideologies. However, multiparty systems provide greater opportunity for people of all backgrounds and ideologies to be democratically represented in the State (Hafez, 2021). This is particularly important in very ethnically diverse societies such as the United States. Voter turnout in the United States tend to trend downward and trails behind most other high-income countries. Lyon Nishizawa (2022) writes in the article "How Does U.S. Voter Turnout Compare to the Rest of the World's?" that "low turnout has been a feature of U.S. politics for the past century, with presidential elections consistently bringing out between 50 and 65 percent" (para. 5). There are a litany of explanations and speculations as to why voter turnout is so low in the United States, but we will review just a couple significant causes. The first explanation for low voter turnout is voter disenfranchisement. **Voter disenfranchisement** can be defined as depriving a citizen of access to or the right to vote. We should remember that those incarcerated in the United States are still citizens, although about 4.6 million of those behind bars are barred from voting due to a felony conviction (Uggen et. al., 2022). Felony disenfranchisement laws are one example among many of legislation that has been passed throughout the country that systematically prevents large swaths of certain populations from voting. Throughout the Jim Crow period of U.S. history, poll taxes and literacy test requirements served the function of preventing most Black Americans from voting. At the time of this writing, at least 36 states request or require identification from voters. These voter ID laws may require a voter to present photo identification, a signature, and/or a piece of mail with their current name and address. Some polling locations reserve the right to restrict voting if acceptable identification is not provided (National Conference of State Legislators [NCSL], 2023). Voter ID laws are particularly disadvantageous to young, poor, and unemployed voters. They also perpetuate the state's tracking and recordkeeping of personal information. In practice, voter disenfranchisement can also take the form of one single day to cast votes, long lines at voting polls, or voter intimidation tactics.

The next explanation for low voter turnout in the United States that I will offer is voter apathy. **Voter apathy** is indifference on the part of individuals with respect to the political process of voting. It is a myth that only the poorly educated and less informed decline voting. They may make up more of the nonvoting collective in most elections, due in part to the issues of disenfranchisement previously discussed, but also due to higher levels of voter apathy. Historical trends have shown a decrease in significant differences between the actions of the two dominant political parties in the United States. Although Democrats and Republicans tend to take different stances on national issues such as minimum wage, paid paternity leave, and how much the government should fund social welfare programs, they are almost unanimously aligned on geopolitical issues. Some of the issues that have the most bipartisan alignment include economic and political support for financial institutions and corporations, continuous expansive funding for the military and law enforcement, and sanctions and military actions toward various countries around the world. In recent years, general members of the American public have awakened to the ways in which the world's countries are interdependent and that they share the consequences of crises such as climate change, war, and health pandemics.

Voters in the United States are also apathetic about the candidates put forward in presidential elections. As of 2023, we have yet to see a woman president, a Muslim president, or queer president elected in the United States. Although according to the U.S. Constitution, the requirements for president are only that the person be at least 35 years of age, be a natural-born citizen, and must have lived in the United States for at least 14 years, all U.S. presidents have been men. They have not only been men, but most are also middle to upper-class, tall, Christian men. This is not happenstance. The notion that men are best suited for positions of authority and decision-making is pervasive in U.S. culture. This is also a country that continues to deal with significant issues of racism, classism, sexism, homophobia, and Christian ideological dominance. These issues are compounded by the contradictions and consequences of capitalism and imperialism. It is difficult to obtain a body of representative electorates when most of the individuals who make it into the Congress, Senate, and presidential cabinets are (or become) millionaires who are bestowed excellent health insurance plans. Not only do most members of the three major branches of government not represent the demographic characteristics and life experiences of the masses of people in the United States, but they also fail to reflect the will of the people. It is in this way that a presumably democratic society operates like that of a **plutocracy** in which society is governed by the wealthy and the interests of the wealthy. Sociologist C. Wright Mills (1956) referred to this phenomenon as a **power-elite model**, a social model in which the upper-class hold most of society's wealth, power, and prestige. Mills argued that the power-elite are in charge of the three major sectors of society: the government, the military, and the economy. A fundamental aspect of the power-elite model is that those at the top are so powerful that they face no real opposition from the public. It is not that they are not ever contested or opposed, but that they yield the power to contain, control, and sanction dissent. This is oppositional to democratic freedom because it leaves little room for checks and balances.

MAJOR ECONOMIC SYSTEMS OF THE WORLD

It may surprise some people to know that there are only a few different types of economic systems that operate in the world today, and that most are mixed economies.

Mixed Economies

Although all societies that have existed in human history have had some form of an economic system, the evolution of industrialization brought about more intricate and full spectrum systems. Contemporarily, there are two basic types of economic systems: capitalist systems and socialist systems. However, most economic systems, ranging from Tanzania to France, have a mixture of these two types, with one type playing a more central role. Even in the

United States, which is probably the clearest example of a capitalist economic system, taxes paid by all citizens pay for road maintenance, parks, and public safety. Additionally, the U.S. government budget allocates funds for things such as infrastructure development and maintenance and owns and operates businesses such as the U.S. Postal Service and Amtrak railroad system. Some countries with predominantly capitalist economies refer to themselves as democratic-socialist to characterize the blended nature of their economy. Democratic socialism can be described as a system in which social and economic decisions are made collectively by use of democratic political processes. Private property and profit are not eliminated but are not concentrated among the wealthiest in society. Many countries around the world have democratic socialist economies, such as Ireland, Sweden, Spain, and Canada. Features of democratic socialism can include a redistribution of income through progressive tax plans that are based on one's ability to pay, tax money used toward nationalized education, health and medical care, pensions, paid family leave, and sometimes housing. Instead of private profit being the focal point of the economic structure, the collective well-being of the society is principal (Ballantine & Roberts, 2012). It is difficult to find a perfect balance between market and collective economies and most inevitably lean in either direction.

Capitalist Systems

Capitalism has three primary features: (a) private ownership of property, (b) pursuit of personal profit, and (c) competition and consumer choice. When it comes to private ownership, individuals can own anything from companies to real estate, to natural resources. Profit is the paramount motive and orientation of a capitalist system. Making money, and as much as you can, is seen as a natural and expected way of life. A purely capitalist economy would have a free-market system in with little to no government regulation. In this way we see that the United States does not have a purely capitalist economy since the government oversees and determines the federal minimum wage for laborers, taxes citizens based on their income, and enforces workplace safety standards (Macionis, 2015). However, those with private ownership of the means of production benefit from a minimum wage, which allows them to maximize labor output to bring in more profit than the cost of expenditures. Over the last few decades, we have witnessed the outsourcing of industry and labor to less affluent countries around the world in order for multinational corporations to pay the least amount in wages with fewer restrictions on their operations and standards. Karl Marx and Frederick Engels argued in the *Communist Manifesto* (1848) that capitalism would split society into two economic classes: the *bourgeoisie*, the owners of the means of production, and the *proletariat*, those who work for the capitalists. This division would eventually lead to class conflict and warfare led by workers who realize their predicament, develop political consciousness, and revolt against their conditions. According to Marx and Engels, this revolution would lead to the development of a new social order, **communism**, in which the class system is eliminated, the means of production are collectively owned, and everyone shares the benefit of labor equally.

Socialist Systems

Marx and Engels (1848) believed that the elimination of capitalism would lead to socialism, which would progress to communism. There is currently no society in the world that is purely communist, but many are socialist with communist characteristics or aspirations. **Socialism** is an economic system characterized by these primary features: (a) collective ownership of property, (b) pursuit of collective goals, and (c) government control of the economy. In a socialist economy, private property may not be altogether eliminated but it would have limitations, particularly on property that generates income. Goods and services are available to all, not just those who can afford it. The collective orientation of socialism emphasizes pursuit of goals that are in the best interests of all in the society. Government regulation of the economy makes obsolete things like commercial advertising and corporate pursuits of profit. However, this does not mean that everyone is poor. In fact, poverty and homelessness is a lot less common in socialist countries due to the lack of competition for wealth and efforts to meet the needs of all. Of course, this also means that there are little to no ultra-rich capitalists. Although socialism faced a steep decline in the 1990s after the dissolution of the Soviet Union and the move of countries in Eastern Europe toward a market economy, today dozens of nations around the world have socialist economic models, including Vietnam, Cuba, the Democratic Republic of Korea (or North Korea), Tanzania, and Venezuela.

THE GEOPOLITICS OF DEVELOPMENT

In Chapter 5, we examined world systems theory and other conceptions about how countries develop, why some are underdeveloped, and how development can be advanced. Now we will briefly explore how geopolitics shapes development. As previously mentioned, development does not only include industrial, technological, and scientific development. Social and cultural development are also important facets that shape the operation of societies. Many countries that are low income or less economically affluent are rich in culture and social relations. For example, although Cuba is a relatively low-income country (largely due to a 60-plus year economic blockade), the preservation of cultural diversity is central to its inhabitants. Music and dancing are common across cities in Cuba. Visitors become familiar with some of Cuba's heroes and revolutionaries due to the visibility of art and posters that display their images and quotes. Cultural celebrations are invested in by the government and taken very seriously by Cubans. For example, in 2022 over 5 million Cubans celebrated May Day throughout the country. In Havana alone, more than 700,000 workers and students attended the parade led by the slogan "Cuba Works and Lives" (Branan, 2022). Five million people may not seem like much in a country like the United States, with a population of over 300 million people. However, for Cuba's population of 11 million, 5 million people make up almost half of the entire population.

Many are surprised when they visit some countries in the Global South and east and notice a lot less homelessness and poverty than what one will find in any given major U.S. city. One must also ask and attempt to answer the question "Why are countries that are so rich in natural resources so economically poor?" For instance, the Democratic Republic of Congo has the second largest rainforest in the world in its Basin region and is abundant in resources such as timber, gold, and iron-ore. Yet, the World Bank ranks it as one of the top five low-income nations in the world. Is it because Africans just cannot get themselves together, or is there a more honest assessment to be had? We must acknowledge that for centuries the countries of Western Europe enslaved people and colonized the land of most countries in Africa, Asia, and Latin America. One can actually count on both hands the number of countries in the Global South and East that were never colonized! After the period of formal colonization ended a neocolonial period begin and endures in the present. International financial organizations like the World Bank and the International Monetary Fund have played a significant role in the underdevelopment or stagnated development of countries that have accepted their loans. The amount of the loans themselves are an impediment, as most countries can never repay them, not even the interest that is accumulated. Thus, they enter a never-ending debt cycle that often leads to further impoverishment. Furthermore, these financiers require countries to accept austerity measures, which often include pension and Social Security reforms, labor reforms, adjustments to public sector wages, and the privatization of public assets. Each of these measures further exacerbate poverty and social inequalities (Bretton Woods Project, 2022). Neocolonialism operates in various ways from countries such as Jamaica and the Bahamas, which are still under the control of the Commonwealth of Britain, or the 14 African nations that use the CFA franc and are therefore in economic servitude to France, their former colonizer. According to an article by Louati (2023),

> Given the vast disparities between African and French economies, the pegging of the region's currency to a strong currency like the French Franc yesterday and the euro today is unnatural and has direct implications on the economic development of the CFA Franc region: reduction in liquidity when governments need it, penalties in exports, reduced the margin for central banks to intervene, which in turn makes them focused solely on fighting inflation and not economic development, the scarcity of investment money for businesses and households face prohibitive interest rates. (para. 9)

A country's development has a lot to do with their history in relation to slavery and colonization, the racial/ethnic composition of their population, their economic trade and finance agreements, and their means of production. These factors are as much geographical as they are political.

THE EMERGENCE OF MULTIPOLARITY

As illustrated in the opening vignette of the chapter, power relations in the world are shifting. These political shifts are referred to as **multipolarity**, shared economic and political power across a variety of nations. More specifically, multipolarity is an anti-imperial arrangement in which countries have autonomy and sovereignty and are not dictated by more powerful countries. Advances toward multipolarity include countries deciding to use local currencies instead of that of dominant countries in the Western hemisphere, alternative international finance organizations, and resistance struggles aimed at removing the residuals of colonization and enslavement. Economist Radhika Desai (2015) posits that multipolarity can be traced back to the 1870s with the industrialization of the United States, Germany, and Japan, which halted the preeminence of the United Kingdom. Although the United Kingdom and other countries in western Europe were doing quite well at that time, due to the profits of slavery, most countries outside of the Western hemisphere were still shedding the shackles of slavery and land colonization.

But in the 1870s the United States was not the global powerhouse that it is today. We have addressed the dominance of the U.S. dollar in global trade relations, but the U.S. also has the largest and most highly funded military, is one of five permanent members of the United Nations Security Council and has the most voting power and financial contribution to the World Bank and International Monetary Fund. However, today China is arguably the top manufacturer in the world and has the second largest gross domestic product (GDP) after that of the United States. China's president Xi Jinping has said on more than one occasion that China would "never seek global hegemony" and would not develop "at the expense of other countries' interests" (Wang, 2018, para. 6). To again reiterate the words of economist Radhika Desai (2015), the study of geopolitical economy, "is better able to understand the multipolar world, reconstruct its historical evolution, and assess its progressive potential" (para. 2).

Applying Sociology: Examine a Country Through a Geopolitical Economy Lens

Choose a country and write a summary that includes the following:

1. Provide some demographic information about the country such as population size, racial/ethnic composition, sex/gender composition, social class distribution, languages spoken, occupations, and so on.
2. How does the country fair as far as educational attainment, gender equality, health outcomes, and life expectancy?

Image 10.2

3. What is significant about the land or geography of the country? What natural resources does the country have? Are the resources extracted, manufactured, and/or imported or exported? Explain.
4. What is the level of industrial development in the country? Is its economic base agricultural, industrial, or technological? Explain.
5. What is the political system of the country? How is the country governed? What options for political engagement exist? Would you consider the country powerful? Why or why not? Is the country sovereign? Why or why not?

SUMMARY: CONNECTING THE PIECES

In this chapter we approached politics and the economy as interconnected systems that are shaped by geography. An analysis of geopolitical economy helps us to better understand global power relations and why and how countries develop. We understand that development is not only economic, but political, social, and cultural. A foundational component of the sociological perspective is to be able to connect history to the present. Social phenomenon in the contemporary world is shaped by what has occurred in the past. The legacy of past actions, migrations, and struggles have residual impact on our lives today. The world will continue to change, and from all indications it will change in transformative ways. As the world advances toward multipolarity, we can expect significant social, economic, political, and cultural shifts.

REVIEW AND CRITICAL THINKING

Directions: Respond to the questions and prompts, based on what you have learned in this chapter:

1. Choose one of the key terms from the chapter and apply it to a real-world example.
2. If you had to describe geopolitical economy to a friend, what information would you provide?
3. Discuss some of the key differences between the major political systems of the world.
4. Discuss some of the key differences between the major economic systems of the world.
5. What geopolitical factors should be considered when assessing a country's development?
6. What is multipolarity? Provide two examples.

Credits
IMG 10.1: Copyright © 2014 Depositphotos/Frankljunior.
IMG 10.2: Copyright © 2010 Depositphotos/Elnur_.

■ **CHAPTER 11**

Education and Religion

HOW SEPARATE ARE CHURCH AND STATE?

The separation of church and state is both a legal and philosophical doctrine that denotes a detachment between religions organizations and the state. This proclamation was first brought forward in the Establishment Clause of the First Amendment to the Constitution of the United States, which prohibited the government from making any law that

Image 11.1

established a religion. It was reinforced in the Supreme Court case *Everson v. Board of Education*, (1947) in which Court Justice Hugo Black asserted that the Establishment Clause means that "neither a State nor the federal government can set up a church. Neither can pass laws which aid one religion, aid all religions, or prefer one religion over another. Neither can force nor influence a person to go to or to remain away from church against their will or force them to profess a belief or disbelief in any religion. No person can be punished for entertaining or professing religious beliefs or disbeliefs, for church attendance or non-attendance" (Cornel Law School, 2022, para. 1).

However, in practice church and state do not tend to be so separate. The clearest examples of this are U.S. dollars with the printed phrase "In God We Trust" and the recurrent utterances of "God Bless America" at public events, ceremonies, and in media programs. Although most people who are religiously affiliated in the United States identify with some denomination of Christianity, most Americans oppose the declaration of any religion as the official faith of the United States (Pew Research Center, 2021). This is one area of many in the social arena in which political divisions exist. According to the same Pew Research Center study, more Republicans than Democrats say they want a more prominent place for Christianity in U.S. national identity. According to Ian Philbrick (2022), author of *The New York Times* article "A Pro-Religion Court," "Over the past few decades, the rise of the religious right has made religious freedom a political priority for Republicans" (para. 6). Philbrick writes that this shift toward Court justices that are pro-religion is a result of selection and succession, in which Republican-appointed justices time their retirements to ensure that a Republican president will name their successor. Court Justice Samuel Alito is one such person who has benefited from well-timed departures. Justice Alito is one of five Court justices to overturn the historic *Roe v. Wade* abortion law stating that the original law was "egregiously wrong" and "deeply damaging" (NPR, 2022, para. 2). In his speech to the Notre Dame Law School's Religious Liberty Initiative held in Rome from July 20–22, 2022, Alito stated that the "turn away from religion" was detrimental and that there needs to be "fight against secularism" (Wehle, 2022, para. 3).

One must consider whether it is even possible to separate church from state when many of those that govern the United States hold religious (specifically Christian) beliefs. Beliefs inevitably shape our choices no matter how objective one tries to be, especially when those choices are believed to be moral. Religion has some role or influence in all social institutions in the United States, even the institution of education. Most explicit are parochial and faith-based schools, but even in public schools, Christian prayers and phrases are customary during graduation ceremonies and sports events. Religious affiliation is not bad in and of itself, but a sociological analysis takes into consideration the way that religion creates social hierarchies and creates and reinforces systems of privilege and oppression.

✓ CHAPTER OBJECTIVES

After completing this chapter students should be able to do the following:

✔ **Discuss** education and religion as social institutions.

✔ **Describe** some of the tensions and contradictions between education, democracy, and capitalism.

✔ **Explain** education from the perspective of one of the major sociological theories.

✔ **Explain** religion from the perspective of one of the major sociological theories.

✔ **Compare and contrast** the major religions of the world.

✔ **Discuss** the political nature of religion in society.

KEY TERMS

education
schooling
credentialism

monotheism
polytheism
reincarnation

religiosity

EDUCATION AS A SOCIAL INSTITUTION

In Chapter 4, social institutions were described as organized sets of structures established to meet the fundamental survival needs of society and provide guidelines for behavior. Social institutions are the pillars of a society and carry out its primary functions. **Education** is a social institution that facilitates the development of a person by providing knowledge, technical skills, and an understanding of cultural norms and values. We can learn a lot of these same things from relatives, friends, and coworkers, who show that education can take place inside and outside of formal institutions. When education takes place in a formal institution of learning it is referred to as **schooling**, formal instruction carried out by trained and credentialed teachers. In 1918, all U.S. states passed *mandatory education laws* that required children to attend school until the age of 16 or the completion of eighth grade (Macionis, 2015). Currently, schooling is still compulsory, but when one can discontinue varies by state and ranges from 14 to 18 years.

The institution of education contains various groups and organizations such as grade-based primary schools, colleges, universities, sports teams, unions, and various associations. Status positions held within educational groups and organizations include teachers, students, principals, department heads, and deans. Each status is associated with particular roles, duties, and expectations. While schooling provides information about a society's cultural norms and values, the institution of education has its own norms and values. They can include values like achievement and success and norms such as doing homework, preparing lectures, and serving on committees. Since no social institution operates in isolation, education is shaped and influenced by other institutions, culture, and the demographics of a society.

EDUCATION, DEMOCRACY, AND CAPITALISM

We previously discussed the institutions of politics and the economy and will not connect them with the institution of education. One of the stated democratic values of the United States is an educated or informed citizenry. This is another concept conferred by Thomas Jefferson that has been transmitted throughout out U.S. culture and institutions ever since. Jefferson addressed the need for educating the "republic" on several occasions with statements such as "It is highly interesting to our country, and it is the duty of its functionaries, to provide that every citizen in it should receive an education proportioned to the condition and pursuits of his life" (Jefferson, 1814, para. XX) and "A system of general instruction, which shall reach every description of our citizens from the richest to the poorest, as it was the earliest, so will it be the latest of all the public concerns in which I shall permit myself to take an interest" (Jefferson, 1818, para. XX). These two quotes illustrate that Jefferson felt education should be something provided to and accessible by the general population (not necessarily the enslaved) regardless of economic status. He felt that an educated and informed citizenry is what sustained a society and kept it functional. Today, education can be directly linked to an individual's job options and income. Although many people may believe that education is a right for everyone in society, in practice schooling has become a major source of social class division. Although public educational institutions receive some amount of government funding, another portion of funding is drawn from property taxes. Since neighborhoods and communities tend to be ethnically and economically homogenous, wealthier communities have better funded schools that can provide more material resources and pay teachers and staff better wages. Research on schooling shows that income segregation in school districts directly contributes to gaps in achievement—test scores and graduation rates (Kozol, 2011; Owens, 2018).

There are also the contradictions of capitalism that must be weighed. Education, like most social institutions in the United States, seeks to generate profit; therefore, the economically affluent have an advantage. Although public schools are tuition free in the United States, there are various costs associated with enrollment such as field trips, involvement in some sports teams, yearbook purchases, class photo purchases, and so forth. These things may not be required of public school students, but they are offered and viewed as a normative part of the schooling experience. Of course, institutions of higher education do require admission and tuition fees, which prevent many potential students from attending these schools (Dickler, 2021). Not only do the most "prestigious" colleges and universities demand higher test scores and GPAs than other institutions, but they are also significantly more expensive. The mythology that college is something that everyone does operates heavily throughout the country, but not only is everyone not able to attend college, many that do will not complete. According to the U.S. Census Bureau (2022) educational attainment data (2022), about 14.3% of adults in the United States hold an advanced degree. It is worth noting that the value of college degrees has changed, and many forms of work no longer require or need employees with advanced degrees. However, **credentialism**, in which employers use educational credentials as screening devices for sorting through pools of applicants, is still a common practice in most traditional workplaces. The student loan debt crisis has shown us that the cost of higher education is a problem for people across demographics. Neither loans, grants nor scholarships have been adequate in closing the class disparities of schooling. It is something that must be addressed systemically, beginning with continuous and substantive conversations about whether higher education should carry a cost at all in a democratic society.

MAJOR RELIGIONS OF THE WORLD

There are thousands of religions present in the world. Some are formal and organized; others are more psychic and spiritual. There are traditional, Indigenous, and folk religious and spiritual practices in which millions of people around the world engage. Here, we will discuss the development and primary beliefs and practices of three of the most popular *organized* religions: Christianity, Islam, and Hinduism. It is also important to note that increasingly people are unaffiliated with any religion. According to the Pew Research Center (2015), it is estimated that by 2050 over 1.2 billion people will be religiously unaffiliated.

Christianity

Christianity, which is believed to be an extension of or development out of Judaism, is based on the belief that Jesus Christ is the Messiah, or God promised to the Jews. Christians today believe that by extension Jesus is the Savior for all that believe in Him. Although Christianity is considered a **monotheistic** religion (belief in only one God), Christians believe in the Father (God), the Son (Jesus Christ), and the Holy Spirit (God's power). This is often referred to as the *trinity*, although the word does not appear in most versions of the Bible. The story of Jesus is that he was born to a virgin mother (Mary) and therefore conceived miraculously. Around 30 years of age, Jesus began a preaching and healing ministry and gained 12 disciples and numerous followers. Since his teachings and miracles challenged prior religious establishment, a plot for his murder was derived and carried out. Christians interpret the death of Jesus as sacrifice for the sins of humanity. Therefore, all that believe in Him and His doctrine will have eternal life in heaven as long as they try to avoid sin and pray for forgiveness when sins are committed.

Today, Christianity is the most populous organized religion in the world, with over 2.2 billion followers (Henslin, 2019). Although most Christians share the foundational beliefs of the religion, there are thousands of denominations of Christianity and hundreds of versions of the Bible.

Islam

Those who follow the religion of Islam are called Muslims, which translates in Arabic as those who submit to God (Allah). The holy book in Islam is called the Qur'an, and it is believed that the last Prophet of Allah, Muhammad, was orally told the content of the Qur'an by the angel Gabriel over a 23-year period. Muhammad recited the Qur'an, and it was documented and transmitted by others. Muhammad was born in Mecca and orphaned at an early age. He was raised primarily by his grandfather and uncle. Muhammad was poor and illiterate, which made it difficult for many to believe that he had been given revelations from Allah. The disbelief in his prophecy so enraged some that, like Jesus, a plot for his murder was arranged. Muhammad fled to Medina for safety, where he was better received and able to accumulate a steady number of followers of Islam. It was in Medina that he was able to establish an Islamic government, which was mimicked in Mecca upon his return years later. Muslims are obligated to make a pilgrimage to Mecca at least once in their life if possible. After Muhammad died at the age of 61 from illness, a struggle ensued over the Meccan empire. Islam was thus split into two major branches that remain today, Sunni and Shi'ite. Sufi Muslims are another branch of Islam that make up the smallest portion of the Islamic community. There are some differences in rituals and legal traditions among these groups.

Like Christianity and Judaism, Islam is considered an Abrahamic religion, one that traces its lineage to the prophet Abraham. Abraham's son Ishmael had 12 sons from whom a significant portion of today's "Arab world" is descended. Muslims consider the Torah of the Jews and the Bible of the Christians sacred but believe that the Qur'an is the ultimate and final word of Allah. For Muslims Jesus (called *Isa* in Arabic) is a beloved prophet, but not God or an offspring of God. Islam is said to be the fastest growing religion in the world, with over 1.5 billion followers at the time of this writing (Henslin, 2019).

Hinduism

Hinduism is thought to be over 10,000 years old and has been the primary religion of India (the most populous country in the world) for at least the last 3,000 years. Hinduism has no specific founder or particular scripture or doctrine—thus no texts "inspired by God." There are several books that Hindus use as guides on moral qualities for people to strive to develop and embody. The books also describe sacrifices that should be made to the gods. Hindus are **polytheists**, meaning that they believe there are many gods. They believe that one god, Brahma, created the universe and that a triad of gods are central to Hinduism: Brahma, Shiva (the Destroyer), and Vishnu (the Preserver). A central belief of Hinduism is in the concept of *karma*, a spiritual progression in which beneficial effects are derived from past beneficial actions and harmful effects from past harmful actions. Instead of death and a final judgement by God, Hindus believe in **reincarnation**, a succession of rebirths after death. While death may take the body, the soul remains and returns in a form aligned with the individual's morality in the previous life. Once individual spiritual perfection is reached (nirvana), the cycle of death and rebirth ends, and the soul is reunited with the universal soul. There are over 1 billion followers of Hinduism in the world today (Gupta, 2020; Henslin, 2019).

THE POLITICS OF RELIGION

Religion is not only personal and collective, but it also connected to power structures within a society. Its manifestation both shapes and is shaped by society. Since religion is foremost a system of beliefs, it guides the behavior of its adherents and therefore impacts the lives of everyone. It has been illustrated that Christianity is the most populous religion in the United States and the religious affiliation of many individuals that hold positions of power in the country. In this way, religion is a political institution, and the determinations that stem from its beliefs are politically charged. Religion operates as form of social stratification in which those who are a part of the dominant religious group occupy a higher stratum of the socio-religious hierarchy. In the United States, Christianity is the religious standard upon which other religions are assessed. The degree of difference from Christianity that a religion exhibits can subject its followers to scrutiny, ridicule, or even physical harm.

Although the First Amendment to the U.S. Constitution states that citizens have the right to religious freedom, and Title VII of the Civil Rights Act of 1964 prohibits employment discrimination based on religion, all religious affiliations are not weighted equally. While most denominations of Christianity are widely accepted in the United States, other groups and their religious practices have not been as well received. For years, both FIFA, the International Football Association, and FIBA, the International Basketball Federation, banned head coverings such as hijabs, turbans, kippahs, and yarmulkes for athletes in the associations. This prevented numerous Muslim, Sikh, and Jewish players from taking part in soccer and basketball at a professional level (Fuchs, 2017; Olow, 2019). Most people are aware of the "Muslim ban" put in place by Donald Trump during his presidency that was upheld by the U.S. Supreme Court. You can find an assortment of news stories that describe attacks on Sikh men in which their turbans are knocked from their heads. Most public facilities and workplaces do not accommodate the need for Muslims to make their five daily prayers, and although many prisoners do not eat pork for religious reasons, pork remains a staple food in prisons in the United States (Starr, 2015). The fact that is easier to be Christian than not in the United States and that practicing a non-Christian religion can be cumbersome or even dangerous makes religion a political entity.

Applying Sociology: Connecting Views on Education and Religion to Theory

Do some research looking into government and public positions on issues such as (a) student loan debt cancellation, (b) critical race theory, (c) religious holiday observances in schools, and (d) prayer in school or at school events. Drawing from the table on the following page, decide which of the major sociological perspectives on education and religion best illustrate the government/public position on the issue. Provide an explanation for your selection.

THEORETICAL PERSPECTIVES ON EDUCATION AND RELIGION

Theoretical Perspective	View of Education	View of Religion	Questions to Consider
Functionalist	Schooling contributes to society's stability, solidarity, and cohesion and provides opportunities for upward mobility.	Religion provides meaning and purpose for lives for some. Religion can unify people. Religion can be a mechanism of personal and social control.	What are some of the manifest and latent functions of schooling and organized religion?
Conflict	Schooling reproduces and reinforces social stratification based on variables such as class, race, and gender.	Religion can support social inequalities by constructions of right and wrong ways to live.	How does schooling limit equal opportunity? How does organized religion reinforce social inequalities?
Feminist	Schooling reinforces conventional notions of gender through hiring, language, curriculum, and the organization of activities and events.	Organized religion has gender divisions and hierarchies, many of which subordinate women.	How do religious doctrine and educational curriculums teach ideas about sex and gender?
Symbolic interaction	Schooling teaches cultural roles and values through interactions and practices.	Religion is given sacred meaning through symbols, interpretations, and rituals.	How do curriculums, teachers, and interactions affect students' educational experiences? How does the use and placement of religious symbols shape their sacred meaning?

FIGURE 11.1 *Theoretical Perspectives on Education & Religion*

SUMMARY: CONNECTING THE PIECES

Education and religion are institutions and manifestations that provide some of the most significant human experiences for many people. Both contain an element of learning, study, and personal development. They are enriched in collective spaces through social interactions that generate and reinforce value and meaning. As U.S. society and the global society continue to transform, our views and practices on education and religion will also shift and adapt. Although the employment value of advanced degrees has decreased, it is unlikely that people will discontinue pursuing higher education. Credentialism and meritocracy are powerful concepts that permeate U.S. culture and shape ideas about education, but so do inscribe democratic values. While there has been a notable decline in religious affiliation in the United States, religious affiliation is still quite high among people in other parts of the world that comprise about 96% of the world's population. **Religiosity**, or strong religious or spiritual beliefs, also remain high in the United States. There is no doubt that humans will continue to search for understanding in an increasingly complex and swiftly changing world. Some may do this through schooling, and others may look to faith for inspiration and hope.

REVIEW AND CRITICAL THINKING

Directions: Respond to the questions and prompts, based on what you have learned in this chapter:

1. Discuss some of the inequalities that exist in schooling that are said to be based on equality.
2. Summarize the relationship between education and democracy.
3. Describe how capitalism shapes the institution of education and process of schooling.
4. What are some of the functions and dysfunctions of religion?
5. Discuss how religion influences other social institutions in the United States.
6. Discuss the origins and major tenets of Christianity, Islam, and Hinduism.

Credit
IMG 11.1: Copyright © 2005 by Chris Phan (CC BY 2.0) at https://commons.wikimedia.org/wiki/File:The_intersection_of_Church_and_State_(78728221).jpg.

■ CHAPTER 12

Social Change: Population Dynamics, Land, and Climate Change

A SOCIOLOGICAL WORLDVIEW REVISITED

"The only lasting truth is change" is the proverb of Lauren Olamina, the protagonist of Octavia Butler's book *Parable of the Sower* (1993). The trajectory of history seems to support Lauren's popular phrase. Change appears to be inevitable. But what generates change? How do some of the most transformative

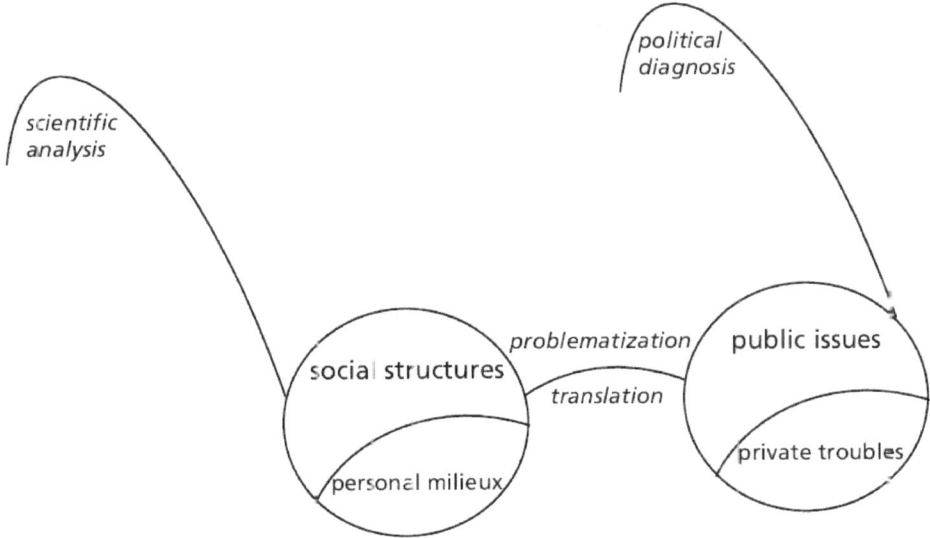

Image 12.1

changes happen? In order to understand social change, we have to understand the mechanisms of society and the variants of human populations. According to C. Wright Mills (1959: 6), the sociological imagination "enables us to grasp history and biography and the relations between the two in society." As sociologists, we must draw from history to understand present-day phenomenon.

Our analysis of historical trajectory is shaped by who writes or transmits the history we learn and how that information is gauged and shaped by our individual identities and experiences. Mills goes on to write that the sociological imagination distinguishes between "the personal troubles of milieu" and "the public issues of social structure" (1959: 8). While our personal problems are shaped by (and in some cases originate from) social structures and institutions, we should not form an analysis of the world that is completely subjective. The "issues of social structure" are issues that impact masses of people. There are also much smaller collectives of people who hold the power to make decisions for the masses. The "power elite" as Mills calls them in his 1956 book of the same name, have interwoven interests that direct their policies, legislation, social structuring, and distribution of public resources. These leaders of the military, corporate, and political elements of society exert an almost totalitarian power in what is stated to be a democratic society.

The sociological bifocals are a reminder of the promise of sociology, the provision of a distinct perspective that accounts for changes over time and the mediation of human populations and the natural environment by and within networks of power. This lens does not develop naturally for most individuals. The typical process of human socialization is standardized and culturally specific. It does not usually emphasis a critical analysis of the society in which we live or encourage us to question our perceptions and conditions. The sociological imagination offers a complimentary worldview that allows us to extend beyond our personal frameworks and become participants in the making of history.

Throughout this text we have examined the foundational concepts and theories in the discipline of sociology. Although you may not remember the details of everything that you have learned in years to come, hopefully the seed of the sociological imagination has been planted and will be nourished and propagated over the course of your lives. The culture of individualism in the United States often leads us to believe that we are autonomous beings who can do everything on our own. We certainly have freewill and personal agency, but our sense of self and experiences in life are shaped, if not determined in some cases, by the society in which we live. Ultimately, we are products of our society. C. Wright Mills has asked us to consider the role that history has played in shaping our personal biographies. He offered some important questions for us to reflect on about the society in which we live, its people and its structures. As we begin to think deeply and critically about our social world, we discover that it is a system of interrelated parts and that a dominant culture binds it. Our vision then expands beyond our specific place in the world and we start to see how the entire world is interconnected. More questions emerge about how we have come to our present circumstance and what kinds of organization and actions propel social change.

We conclude the text by addressing these questions. What we perceive as major social changes today will seem commonplace for future generations. They will be inclined, as we have been, to take for granted the personal and collective struggles and sacrifices that affected our present-day rights and freedoms. Through the lens of the symbolic interaction theory, we understand that each day we re-create society through our daily interactions. Sometimes it is organized social movements and personal acts of defiance that shift and mold our social world. While no one can accurately predict exactly what the future will hold, as the protagonist of Octavia Butler's *Parable of the Sower* (1993) proclaimed "the only lasting truth is change."

✔ CHAPTER OBJECTIVES

After completing this chapter students should be able to do the following:

✔ **Distinguish** between social shifts, social reforms, and social transformation.

✔ **Describe** demography and its contribution to understanding populations.

✔ **Explain** some of the factors that contribute to population size.

✔ **Explain** climate change and the current ecological crisis.

✔ **Discuss** decolonization in theory and practice.

✔ **Describe** some of the revolutionary shifts taking place today.

KEY TERMS

social shift	migration	decolonization
social reform	urbanization	revolution
social transformation	red ining	
demography	climate refugees	

UNDERSTANDING SOCIAL CHANGE: SHIFTS, REFORMS, AND TRANSFORMATION

According to journalist and author Malcolm Gladwell (2006), the *tipping point* is "that magic moment when an idea, trend, or social behavior crosses a threshold, tips, and spreads like wildfire" (p. 2). This is one way to interpret how social change is propelled. The stability of society is determined by whether its members are satisfied with existing conditions. When or if they are not, existing conditions are seen as untenable and are brought forward as problems that need to be solved.

Social Shifts

Not every change is a radical one. Some changes happen on the micro level between groups and individuals and do not fundamentally change the structures or systems of a society. **Social shifts** are an example as seek to alter a mechanism or practice within the social structure. This differentiation is not meant to minimize the significance of social shifts. Social shifts impact personal and collective perceptions and those perceptions guide behavior. An example of an important social shift is changes in the language used to describe disabilities and impairments and associated services. These changes have been made within many businesses, workplaces, and school settings. Not all institutions have adopted linguistic changes, nor are they required by law to do so. However, advocacy around disability justice has compelled many organizations to reframe language and support services. For example, the educational institution in which I am employed recently changed the name of an office once called "Disability Services" to "Accessibility Services." This was a slight, but important change that centered on the role and duties of the office as a source of accommodation and averted the centering of disability. Changes like this can be viewed as *people-first language*, language that "puts the person before the disability, and describes what a person has (or needs), not who a person is" (Office of Disability Rights, 2006, para. 2). Accessibility also implies that we can make things more attainable for those with disabilities and impairments. This reflects a social model of disability that suggests that it is society that needs to be fixed, not people with disabilities. This model focuses on impairments and their implications on social and environmental factors (i.e., attitudes, stereotypes, lack of access, and lack of rights). Thus, a disability becomes something imposed on those with a specific impairment because of the ways inventions have been designed and social activities organized to exclude some and accommodate others (Buder & Perry, 2022).

Social Reforms

Social reforms attempt to change a limited aspect of a society, but not to transform or replace current structures or institutions. More recent examples of social reform movements include the modern women's rights movement, labor union movements, and environmental conservation movements. The civil rights movement of the 1950s and 1960s in the United States is a classic example of a movement that sought social reforms. Participants and supporters of the movement strived for civil rights such as racial desegregation, the right to vote, and equal protections under the law. Unlike later Black Power and Black Liberation movements, the civil rights movement did not demand a transformation of the U.S. political system or economic system. Although toward the end of his life and shortly before his assassination, Martin Luther King Jr. shifted his emphasis on civil rights to human rights. He realized that more drastic changes would be needed in order to achieve social equity and racial justice. In one of his last speeches, *Beyond Vietnam* given in 1967, he condemned war and wanted the U.S. government to see the humanity in those deemed "enemies" (2012, p. 48). In a speech that same year called "The Three Evil of Society," he designated racism, poverty, and militarism as the three evils that plague U.S. society. King had concluded that "racial injustice and economic injustice cannot be solved without a radical redistribution of political and economic power (2012, p. 62).

Social Transformation

What Martin Luther King Jr. had realized shortly before his assassination was that social transformation was needed in the United States. Shifts and reforms pursue interests within the existing social system. **Social transformation** involves changing a system or structure so drastically that it becomes something new. Although social transformation may not always involve a violent or combative overthrow of a system, few social transformations in history have happened without it. Social transformation seeks a new social order and new social organization. Legislation enforces and institutionalizes these changes. Norms, values, and other aspects of culture are shaped around it and support it. Examples of social transformations include wars that have led to the establishment of new governments and economic structures such as the Revolutionary War (1775–1783), the Civil War (1861–1865), World War II (1939–1945), and various combats and wars for independence throughout Africa in the 1950s and 1960s. Noncombative transformative changes are possible within basic social institutions, including the labor force or educational institutions. Success can be derived in these institutions from labor strikes, changes in elections, and acts of civil disobedience. However, as previously stated, these kinds of changes do not transform entire systems, they alter some aspects of an existing system.

POPULATION DYNAMICS: HOW DEMOGRAPHICS SHAPE AND PROPEL CHANGE

The world population at the time of this writing is nearly 8 billion! Eight billion people are occupying the Earth's land and relying on its natural resources. Although only about 4% of the world population resides in the United States (about 330 million people), its population exerts a lot of power over the global community and uses more than its share of resources and energy (University of Michigan Center for Sustainable Systems, 2021). The study of population characteristics is called **demography** and is a major area of research in sociology. Demographic data such as population composition, birth and death rates, life expectancy, and patterns of migration help us to better understand social problems and make predictions about the future of a society.

Population Composition

One of the first questions posed by C. Wright Mills (1959) in the essay *The Promise*, from his book "The Sociological Imagination" (1959), is that we consider who lives in a given society and what is happening to them. The composition of the population determines the amount and types of resources needed, where there may be strains, and what variations in thought exist. Demographers and sociologists often examine the age and gender structures of a society to ascertain birth rates, death rates, and life expectancy. We have been able to synthesize some generalizable data and conclude that population growth does not occur evenly across countries. The proportion of older people in the world (over age 65) has steadily grown in places like Japan, Germany, and Italy. While birthrates may be relatively low, life expectancy is increasing. For many countries in the Global South, which includes countries in Latin America, Southeast Asia, and Africa, the age structure is more likely to be dominated by younger people. In many of these countries, birthrates tend to be high, but life expectancy is relatively low (Newman, 2017). From an institutional standpoint, many governments have begun reducing social services for the elderly, such as pensions, to offset the costs of a decreasing number of younger people who are paying into the system. On the opposite end, populations with large numbers of young people have more strained labor markets and education systems. These effects due to the age structure and fertility rates of population impact living standards. Dissatisfaction with declining living standards have led to protests and uprisings all over the world. Although many major uprisings have occurred in countries in the Global South in which a significant portion of the population is under 30 years of age (i.e., Egypt, Syria, Burkina Faso, Mali, Sudan, etc.), we have seen massive labor strikes and protests related to pension reform in countries like France, the United Kingdom, Spain, and Germany (Yanatma, 2023). Social class divisions and contentions, many of which are derived from labor and wages, cut across demographic categories. Most people can clearly understand the importance of economic stability on one's ability to progress and thrive in life. These are issues that will continue to stir and shape social change for years to come.

Patterns of Migration

Migration, or the movement of people from one region to another, is another primary factor in shaping population demographics. Migration can occur within a country, into another country (immigration), or out of a country (emigration). Migration can diversify a population or make it more homogenous. The United States has experienced a few periods of heightened immigration, notably the mass migration of European colonists in the 16th and 17th centuries who colonized what was formerly known as Turtle Island, the importation of millions enslaved Africans, the tens of millions of European immigrants who entered the country in the late 1800s and early 1900s, and immigration from Latin America and Asia post-1965 (Hirschman, 2006). Many immigrants have come to major cities in the United States to find work and to connect with other immigrants. The process by which people concentrate in large cities is referred to as **urbanization**. Today, over half of the world's population lives in cities as opposed to rural areas (Mindich, 2014). While in the United States this does put a strain on housing accommodation and increases competition for quality jobs, we can't ignore the role of corporate inflation and gentrification in the displacement of native inhabitants. Racism and xenophobia have historically played a role in developing and maintaining ethnically and economically homogenous neighborhoods. We know that the discriminatory practices of the Federal Housing Administration, which date back to its establishment in 1934, have heavily shaped current disparities in housing security and wealth by race and ethnicity. The FHA enacted a process of **redlining**, in which mortgages were least likely to be insured in or near predominantly Black neighborhoods. National Public Radio's Terry Gross interviewed Richard Rothstein (2017), author of the book *The Color of Law*, which provides a detailed history of housing discrimination in the United States. A cumulative point from the interview states that "today African American incomes on average are about 60 percent of average White incomes. But African American wealth is about 5 percent of white wealth. Most middle-class families in this country gain their wealth from the equity they have in their homes. So, this enormous difference between a 60 percent income ratio and a 5 percent wealth ratio is almost entirely attributable to federal housing policy implemented through the 20th century" (para. 11). Many early European immigrants were placed in housing formations later called *ghettos* and *shanty towns* among displaced Black and Native groups. However, it was not a lack of care that created poor living conditions; it was governmental neglect and its ensuing poverty. Due to the racialized nature of housing, neighborhoods with larger numbers of people of color tend to have less infrastructure maintenance and less primacy for quality sanitation services and are subject to displacement due to capital development (Norwood, 2021). More and more environmental catastrophes are forcing people to leave their communities or even their countries. This is illustrated by the thousands of people who have been displaced due to polluted water in Flint, Michigan, or Jackson, Mississippi, in the United States, and the millions of **climate refugees** who voluntary or involuntarily migrate due to the impact of sudden or gradual climate-exacerbated disasters.

CLIMATE CHANGE AND ECOLOGICAL CATASTROPHE

It is no secret that a climate crisis is upon us. In recent years we have seen unprecedented increases in heat waves and disasters such as hurricanes, droughts, and floods. The Earth is indeed warming, and these changes are having a dramatic impact on our air, land, and water. *The Guardian* newspaper contributor Oliver Milman (2023) recently wrote an article called "New York City Is Sinking due to Weight of Its Skyscrapers, New Research Finds." As the title suggests the article describes how New York City "is sinking approximately 1-2mm each year on average" (para. 1). There are two stated causes for the gradual sinkage: first, the rise in sea levels due to the world's glaciers melting away and seawater expansion caused by global heating; second, "the extraordinary weight of its vertiginous buildings" (para. 1). This story connects the two classic framings of the climate change narrative, the human, and the ecological aspects. Christian Parenti (2013) writes in his essay "A Radical Approach to the Climate Crisis" that the growth imperative of capitalism conflicts with nature. He goes further to explain how capitalist production, a major contributor to climate change, is citing the U.S. military as the primary transmitter of fossil fuels in the world. This is due to weapons manufacturing and the maintenance of military bases across the globe.

Industrial development and expansion have led to mass deforestation, overfishing, freshwater depletion, and soil erosion, which has resulted in a loss of biodiversity and various chemical contaminations. As stated by the Party for Socialism and Liberation (2022), "Capitalism cannot provide a solution for the climate crisis because capitalism is the crisis" (p. 45). The authors name the private ownership of the means of production and the capitalist energy market as entities that must be transformed in order to begin to repair ecological devastation. By removing the profit motive of energy production by establishing collectively owned social property, people and the planet are placed at the center. Therefore, energy becomes a common resource instead of a commodity. An ambiguous and revolutionary plan is laid out by the authors as a strategy to address the climate crisis, which indeed seems to require dramatic and transformative solutions. The most dramatic solutions are structural and systemic ones that necessitate changes in the means of production. An equally important change needed is a cultural one that reformulates the way that we think about and engage in consumption and use. This is particularly important for those of us who live in the United States, a country that is one of the world's largest consumers of energy.

DECOLONIZATION IN THEORY AND PRACTICE

In previous sections of the text, we reviewed the conceptual basis and applications of colonialism and neocolonialism. Here, an overview of decolonization as a process of radical social change will be provided. Contrary to popular understandings of decolonization, it is not simply a metaphor for things that we want to do to improve ourselves or society. **Decolonization**, as defined by Eve Tuck and K. Wayne Yang (2012), is the repatriation of Indigenous land and life. Decolonization seeks to engage in a historical process of decoupling from the various forms of colonialism—external colonialism, internal colonialism, and settler colonialism. *External colonialism* can include military operations and war fronts. *Internal colonialism* refers to the management of people within the so-called domestic borders of an imperial nation. Internal colonialism can be produced through psychological or external means. *Settler colonialism* will be emphasized here, as it is most relevant in the context of the United States, in which colonizers came to stay and developed a new home in the occupied land.

As previously discussed, there are few countries in the world that do not have a history of colonization. Although some Indigenous groups have been able to regain their land and independence, many continue the struggle for "land back." In what we now call the United States, millions of people native to the land once called Turtle Island were murdered, and their land was either outright taken or gained through questionable treaties. Surviving Indigenous groups were cast into reservations that have produced some of the highest rates of poverty in the country. Economic instability is in part caused by federal government ownership of most tribal lands. Intense government regulation of supposedly sovereign tribal lands has made the purchasing and developing of land difficult for Indigenous residents (Yeagley, 2020).

In recent years a variety of Indigenous groups and their supporters in the United States have fought against the expansion of oil pipelines and oil drilling ventures. In March of 2023 a million letters were sent to the White House to oppose an oil drilling project on Alaska's North Slope. The Willow Project, as it is called, would drill into some 600 million barrels of oil from a national petroleum reserve. Residents, including tribal groups living in the area, have expressed concerns about how drilling would upset ecological habitats and the health and environmental consequences of this long-term project (Nilsen, 2023). When Indigenous groups in the United States are demanding their "land back" they are making claim not only to literal land, but the reclamation of Indigenous cultures and practices. Indigenous protestors seek to teach us to be stewards of the land and protectors of the water. This perspective is anti-capitalist by nature. It juxtaposes the notion that the only purpose for land is to industrialize and develop it. A land-centered and people-centered focus is what makes these efforts part of a decolonial process. It is a friction against the settler colonial paradigm that sees increases in private profit as progress and ignites the flame of a revolutionary social change that transforms both systems and ideologies.

THE REVOLUTION NOW

In the 1988 song "Talkin' Bout a Revolution," Tracy Chapman sings "Don't you know they're talking about a revolution? It sounds like a whisper." Gil Scott Heron (1971) told us that "the revolution will not be televised" (para. XX), and Malcolm Gladwell (2010) doesn't think that it will be tweeted either. A **revolution** sets out to overturn an existing social order, whether it be a government or another social institution, and replace it with something different. Revolution is the ultimate form of transformative social change. There are various stages and phases of a revolutionary process, periods of heightened activity and times of dormancy. I argue that there is a revolution unfolding around the world today. Demands for land to be returned to the Indigenous and calls for reparations have never been so loud in the United States. National surveys continue to indicate deep dissatisfaction with politics and the economy. A new political and economic world order is being formed with the rise of China's economy and the introduction of multiple currencies into the world market. The revolution now aims to re-imagine and reform societies by developing new social systems and governing arrangements. The masses of people around the world are starting to realize that a class war is upon us in which the minority rich siphon more than their share of money, land, and power from the majority. Bills are becoming increasingly less payable, and working conditions are amiss for many now referred to as *essential workers*. Martin Luther King Jr. came to the conclusion that only a revolutionary change could remedy the United States of its major social problems such as racism and poverty. His shift from civil rights to human rights was meant to de-center power and capital and reconsider the inalienable rights of all human beings. King determined that in order for all humans to have the ability to live and progress in beneficial ways, the social system itself would have to change.

Applying Sociology: Birth Year Reflection 🛒

Search online for a newspaper, news story, or popular magazine that was circulated the year you were born.

1. What were some of the major events that took place that year?
2. What was the state of the economy that year?
3. What were some of the social concerns that year?
4. How do you think the population dynamics of the time shaped what was happening in the social realm?
5. How have the major events of that year and period shaped aspects of contemporary social life?

SUMMARY: CONNECTING THE PIECES

We began the book Robeson book as an illustration of what it means to be a global citizen. To be a global citizen is to be concerned with the cultures and social conditions of people and places outside of our home countries and communities. A global citizen engages in critical study and analysis of the social world to better understand what causes problems and how to resolve them. The discipline of sociology provides a lens through which we can examine the world as a social system with interrelated parts. Although sociology is guided by some key theoretical perspectives, we acknowledge the limitations of any single theory of social life. Ultimately, sociology is a discipline with more questions than concrete answers. By using scientific methods, sociologists can generate some worthwhile explanations about why things happen and projections about future developments. While the promise of sociology is not to provide solutions for all the world's problems, it is a discipline that encourages us to examine unchallenged assumptions and question the previously unquestionable. We will often discover the root causes of social issues as we lay bare the inner skeleton of the social system. Hopefully, some of us will use this newly acquired knowledge for positive social change. Nevertheless, the process of critical analysis can be transformative for us as individuals who contribute to a bigger social picture.

REVIEW AND CRITICAL THINKING

Directions: Respond to the questions and prompts, based on what you have learned in this chapter:

1. Discuss some of the "tipping points" that ignite social change.
2. Consider your own carbon footprint. Are there areas of your life in which you may overconsume? Explain.

3. Describe a historical social change that impacts your life presently.
4. Apply one of the major sociological perspectives to the process of social change.
5. What are the consequences of social change? Consider the impact of change at the micro and macro levels.
6. Describe revolutionary change with the use of sociological concepts and real-world examples.

Credits

IMG 12.1: Thomas Kemple and Renisa Mawani, "The Sociological Imagination and its Imperial Shadows," Theory, Culture & Society, vol. 26, no. 7-8. Copyright © 2009 by SAGE Publications. ICN 12.1: Copyright © by Microsoft. Reprinted with permission.

References

Addams, J. (1895). *Hull-House maps and papers: A presentation of nationalities and wages in a congested district of Chicago, together with comments and essays on problems of the social conditions.* Forgotten Books.

Adelman, L. (Producer), & Christine Herbes-Sommers, Llewellyn M. Smith, Tracy Heather Strain (Directors). (2003). *Race: The power of an illusion* [Documentary]. United States: California News Reel.

Aguirre, A., Jr. & Turner, J. (2009). American ethnicity: The dynamics and consequences of discrimination (7th ed.). McGraw-Hill.

Ahmed, I. S. (2020, May 20). *Twenty-year Treasury bond will add to $25 trillion U.S. debt pile.* Reuters. https://www.reuters.com/article/us-health-coronavirus-bonds-20year/twenty-year-treasury-bond-will-add-to-25-trillion-us-debt-pile-idUSKBN22W0RJ

Alatas, F. S. (2014). *Applying Ibn Khaldun: The recovery of a lost tradition in sociology.* Routledge.

Alber, R. (2017, January 27). *Gender equity in the classroom: Some ideas on how to minimize gender bias in our teaching practice and curriculum.* Edutopia. https://www.edutopia.org/blog/gender-equity-classroom-rebecca-alber

Aljazeera. (2023). *France's pension protests and the future of work.* https://www.aljazeera.com/podcasts/2023/1/27/frances-pension-protests-and-the-future-of-work

American Association of University Women. (2022). *The motherhood penalty.* https://www.aauw.org/issues/equity/motherhood/

American Civil Liberties Union. (2008). *Domestic violence and homelessness.* https://www.aclu.org/sites/default/files/field_document/factsheet_homelessness_2008.pdf

Applewhite, A. (2021, June 29). *Let's climb out of the generation trap.* This Chair Rocks Blog. https://www.nextavenue.org/generation-trap/

Arenstein, T., & Neeley, L. (2023). *Despite the blockade Cuba's health care system is extraordinary.* Worker's World. https://www.workers.org/2023/01/68646/

Ballantine, H. J., & Roberts, A. K. (2012). *Our social world: Condensed version* (2nd ed.). SAGE.

Beaubien, J. (2022). *A small island nation has cooked up not 1, not 2 but 5 COVID vaccines. It's Cuba!* National Public Radio. https://www.npr.org/sections/goatsandsoda/2022/02/01/1056952488/a-small-island-nation-has-cooked-up-not-1-not-2-but-5-covid-vaccines-its-cuba

Belsha, K. (2020). *States and cities are banning hair discrimination. Here's how that's affecting schools.* Chalkbeat. https://www.chalkbeat.org/2020/1/16/21121830/states-and-cities-are-banning-hair-discrimination-here-s-how-that-s-affecting-schools

Benokraitis, N. (2014). *Soc3.* Cengage Learning.

Benokraitis, N. V. (2015). *Marriage & families: Changes, choices, and constraints* (8th ed.). Pearson.

Berger, L. P. (1963). *Invitation to sociology: A humanistic perspective.* Doubleday.

Blecha, P. (2004). *Taboo tunes: A history of banned bands and censored songs.* Backbeat Books.

Bourdieu, P. (1986). *The forms of capital.* In J. Richardson (Ed.), Handbook of theory and research for the sociology of education (pp. 241–258). https://home.iitk.ac.in/~amman/soc748/bourdieu_forms_of_capital.pdf

Branan, E. (2022, May 2). *Over 5 million people march on May Day in Cuba, a country of 11 million.* Liberation News. https://www.liberationnews.org/5-million-people-march-on-may-day-in-cuba-a-country-of-11-million/

Bretton Woods Project. (2019, December). *IMF and World Bank complicit in "austerity as new normal," despite availability of alternatives.* https://www.brettonwoodsproject.org/2019/12/imf-and-world-bank-complicit-in-austerity-as-new-normal-despite-availability-of-alternatives/

Brown, A., & Livingston, G. (2017). *Intermarriage in the U.S. 50 Years After Loving v. Virginia.* Pew Research Center. https://www.pewresearch.org/social-trends/2017/05/18/intermarriage-in-the-u-s-50-years-after-loving-v-virginia/the

Brown, K. (2020). *This year, the Women's March wants to be more accessible for those with disabilities.* https://www.allure.com/story/womens-march-2020-accessibility-for-people-disabilities

Brownmiller, S. (1993). *Against our will: Men, women, and rape.* Random House.

Buchanan, L. (2020). *Black Lives Matter may be the largest movement in U.S. history.* The New York Times. https://www.nytimes.com/interactive/2020/07/03/us/george-floyd-protests-crowd-size.html

Buckholz, K. (2021). *The top 10 percent own 70 percent of U.S. wealth.* Statista. https://www.statista.com/chart/19635/wealth-distribution-percentiles-in-the-us/

Buder, S., & Perry, R. (2016, April 12). *The social model of disability explained.* Social Creatures. https://www.thesocialcreatures.org/thecreaturetimes/the-social-model-of-disability

Butler, O. E. (1993). *Parable of the sower.* Four Walls Eight Windows.

Centers for Disease Control and Prevention. (2022). *What are birth defects?* https://www.cdc.gov/ncbddd/birthdefects/facts.html

Chapman, T. (1988). *Talkin' Bout a Revolution.* On Tracy Chapman. Elektra Records.

China Global Television Network. (2023a). *China healthcare: Medical insurance reform to improve usage efficiency.* https://news.cgtn.com/news/2023-02-19/VHJhbnNjcmlwdDcwNjI5/index.html

China Global Television Network. (2023b). *Smart healthcare: China is building a new model of smart health care.* https://news.cgtn.com/news/2022-11-16/VHJhbnNjcmlwdDY5NDg4/index.html

Chung, S. (2021). *Taxing video game virtual currency transactions: Separating those who play for fun from those who play for profit.* Above the Law. https://abovethelaw.com/2021/03/taxing-video-game-virtual-currency-transactions-separating-those-who-play-for-fun-from-those-who-play-for-profit/

Cohen, P. N. (2021). *The family: Diversity, inequality, and social change.* Norton.

Cohn, D., Horowitz, J. M., Minkin, R., Fry, R., & Hurst, K. (2022, March 24). *Financial issues top the list of reasons U.S. adults live in multigenerational homes.* Pew Research Center. https://www.pewresearch.org/social-trends/2022/03/24/financial-issues-top-the-list-of-reasons-u-s-adults-live-in-multigenerational-homes/

Coleman, M. J. & Ganong L. H. (1st ed.). (2014). The Social History of the American family: An Encyclopedia (Vol. 4, pp. 941-943). Sage Publications.

Congressional Research Service. (2021). *The U.S. income distribution: Trends and issues.* https://sgp.fas.org/crs/misc/R44705.pdf

Congressional Research Service. (2022). *The U.S. dollar as the world's dominant reserve currency.* https://crsreports.congress.gov/product/pdf/IF/IF11707#:~:text=About%20half%20of%20international%20trade,nearly%2090%25%20of%20all%20transactions

Cooper, A. J. (1892). Voices from the South. The Aldine Printing House

Cornell Law School. (2022). *Church and state.* https://www.law.cornell.edu/wex/church_and_state

Cunningham, E., Saich, T., & Turiel, J. (2020). *Understanding CCP resilience: Surveying Chinese public opinion through time.* https://ash.harvard.edu/files/ash/files/final_policy_brief_7.6.2020.pdf

Davis, K. (1947). *Extreme isolation.* In Evelyn Reynolds, A Sociology Reader: Foundational Concepts for the Introductory Student (Preliminary Edition), (pgs. 59-67). Cognella Academic Publishing.

Desai, R. (2015). *Geopolitical economy: The discipline of multipolarity.* https://valdaiclub.com/files/10943/

Desilver, D. (2019). *Despite global concerns about democracy, more than half of countries are democratic.* Pew Research Center https://www.pewresearch.org/short-reads/2019/05/14/more-than-half-of-countries-are-democratic/

Desilver, D. (2022). *Turnout in U.S. has soared in recent elections but by some measures still trails that of many other countries.* Pew Research Center. https://www.pewresearch.org/short-reads/2022/11/01/turnout-in-u-s-has-soared-in-recent-elections-but-by-some-measures-still-trails-that-of-many-other-countries/

Dickler, J. (2021, March 14). *Fewer kids are going to college because they say it costs too much.* CNBC. https://www.cnbc.com/2021/03/14/fewer-kids-going-to-college-because-of-cost.html

District of Colombia Office of Disability Rights. (2006). *People first language.* https://odr.dc.gov/page/people-first-language#:~:text=%E2%80%9CPeople%20First%20Language%E2%80%9D%20(PFL,not%20who%20a%20person%20is

Dolan, A. K., & Withorn-Peterson, C. (2022). *Forbes world's billionaires list.* Forbes. https://www.forbes.com/billionaires/

Dzodin, H. (2020). *American exceptionalism is not the only model.* https://news.cgtn.com/news/2020-07-20/American-exceptionalism-is-not-the-only-model--ShEKh7jUAM/index.html

Engels, F., & Marx, K. (1848). *Manifesto of the Communist Party.* Marxists Internet Archive. https://www.marxists.org/archive/marx/works/download/pdf/Manifesto.pdf

Eppard, L. M., & Rank, M. R. (2021). *The "American dream" of upward mobility is broken. Look at the numbers.* The Guardian. https://www.theguardian.com/commentisfree/2021/mar/13/american-dream-broken-upward-mobility-us

Equity Literacy Institute. (2021). *The equity literacy framework.* https://www.equityliteracy.org/equity-literacy

Fasseeh, A., ElEzbawy, B., Adly, W., ElShawawy, R., Mohsen, G., & Abaza, S., ElShalakani, A., & Kaló, Z. (2022). *Healthcare financing in Egypt: A systematic literature review.* Journal of the Egyptian Public Health Association, 97. https://www.ncbi.nlm.nih.gov/pmc/articles/PMC8741917/

Feagin, J. R., & Feagin, B. C. (2011). Racial and ethnic relations (9th ed.). Pearson.

Federal Bureau of Prisons. (2022). *Inmate statistics.* Bureau of Prisons. https://www.bop.gov/about/statistics/statistics_inmate_race.jsp

Feltey, K., & Sutherland, J.-A. (2013). *Cinematic sociology.* SAGE.

Ferree, M. M., & Wade, L. (2019). *Gender: Ideas, interactions, institutions* (2nd ed.). Norton.

Fisher, D. R. (2022). *Lessons learned from the post-George Floyd protests.* Brookings. https://www.brookings.edu/blog/fixgov/2022/07/22/lessons-learned-from-the-post-george-floyd-protests/

Fuchs, C. (2017). *International Basketball Federation votes to end religious head covering ban.* NBC News. https://www.nbcnews.com/news/asian-america/international-basketball-federation-votes-allow-religious-head-coverings-n755381

Garcia, S. (2020). *Remembrance, resilience, and response: Addressing an epidemic of violence against trans and non-binary people.* https://www.aclu.org/news/lgbtq-rights/remembrance-resilience-and-response-addressing-an-epidemic-of-violence-against-trans-non-binary-people

Giddens, A., Duneier, M., Carr, D., & Appelbaum, P. R. (2015). *Essentials of sociology* (5th ed.). Norton.

Gisbert. P. (1952). *The rise of sociology in Latin America.* Sociological Bulletin, 1(2), p. 128.

Gladwell, M. (2002). *The tipping point.* Back Bay Books.

Gladwell, M. (2010). *Small change: Why the revolution will not be tweeted.* The New Yorker. https://www.newyorker.com/magazine/2010/10/04/small-change-malcolm-gladwell

Goffman, E. (1959). *The presentation of self in everyday life.* Doubleday.

Goffman, E. (1961). *Asylums.* Doubleday.

Gore, T. B. (2013). *A forgotten landmark medical study from 1932 by the Committee on the Cost of Medical Care.* Baylor University Medical Center Proceedings, 26(2), 142–143. https://www.ncbi.nlm.nih.gov/pmc/articles/PMC3603728/

Gould, S. J. (1981). *The mismeasure of man.* Norton.

Greene, S. C. (2017). *"Reclaiming my time": Maxine Waters phrase prompts buzz, memes and a gospel song.* USA Today. https://www.usatoday.com/story/news/politics/onpolitics/2017/08/02/maxine-waters-prompts-buzz-memes-reclaiming-my-time/532334001/

Gross, T. (2017, May 3). *A "forgotten history" of how the U.S. government segregated America.* NPR. from https://www.npr.org/2017/05/03/526655831/a-forgotten-history-of-how-the-u-s-government-segregated-america

Gupta, A. (2020). *Which are the top 5 religions of the world in the chronological order of its origin dating back from the oldest to the newest religion?* Medium. https://medium.com/illumination/list-of-top-5-religions-of-the-world-in-the-chronological-order-of-its-origin-dating-back-from-the-afeabccb5116

Guynn, J. (2019). *If you've been harassed online, you're not alone. More than half of Americans say they've experienced hate.* USA Today. https://www.usatoday.com/story/news/2019/02/13/study-most-americans-have-been-targeted-hateful-speech-online/2846987002/

Hafez, N. (2021). *Democratic systems: Two party v. multi-party.* Lebanon Review. https://lebanonlaw-review.org/democratic-systems-two-party-v-multi-party/

Harlow, H., & Harlow, M. (1962). *Social deprivation in monkeys.* W.H. Freeman.

Henslin, J. M. (2019). *Sociology: A down-to-earth approach* (14th ed.). Pearson.

Heron-Scott, G. (1971). *The Revolution Will Not Be Televised.* On Pieces of a Man. Flying Dutchman.

Hilty, B. E. (1st ed). (2011). *Thinking About Schools: A Foundations of Education Reader.* (Vol. 1). Routledge.

Hirschman, C. (2014). *Immigration to the United States: Recent trends and future prospects.* Malaysian Journal of Economic Studies, 51(1), 69–85. https://www.ncbi.nlm.nih.gov/pmc/articles/PMC4302270/

Hoffman, B. (2003). *Health care reform and social movements in the United States.* American Journal of Public Health, 93(1), 75–85. https://www.ncbi.nlm.nih.gov/pmc/articles/PMC1447696/

Hughes, M. & Kroehler, C.J. (2007). Sociology: The Core. McGraw-Hil

International Labor Organization. (2017). *Forced labour, modern slavery, and human trafficking.* https://www.ilo.org/global/topics/forced-labour/lang--en/index.htm

International Labor Organization. (2019). *Afghanistan employment and environmental sustainability fact sheets.* https://www.ilo.org/wcmsp5/groups/public/---asia/---ro-bangkok/documents/publication/wcms_625888.pdf

Intersex Human Rights Australia. (2019). *Intersex population figures.* https://ihra.org.au/166C1/intersex-numbers/

Jacobo, J. (2019). *Teens spend more than 7 hours on screens for entertainment a day: Report.* ABC News. https://abcnews.go.com/US/teens-spend-hours-screens-entertainment-day-report/story?id=66607555

Jefferson, T. (1814). *Thomas Jefferson to Peter Carr, 7 September 1814.* National Archives. https://founders.archives.gov/documents/Jefferson/03-07-02-0462

Jefferson, T. (1818). *Thomas Jefferson to Joseph C. Cabell, 14 January 1818.* National Archives. https://founders.archives.gov/documents/Jefferson/03-12-02-0294

Johnson, A. (2014). *Culture: Symbols, Ideas, and the Stuff of Life.* In Allen G. Johnson, The Forest and the Trees: Sociology as Life, Practice, and Promise (pp. 31–62). Temple University Press.

Johnson, E. M. (2021). *Factbox: Wealth and philanthropy of Bill and Melinda Gates.* Reuters. https://www.reuters.com/business/retail-consumer/wealth-philanthropy-bill-melinda-gates-2021-05-03/

Jurjevich, J. (2021). *Languages spoken at home and Census 2020.* U.S. Census Bureau. https://www.census.gov/acs/www/about/why-we-ask-each-question/language/

King, B. (2014). *Make way for the Wintermaker.* Sky & Telescope. https://skyandtelescope.org/astronomy-blogs/make-way-wintermaker1122014bk/

King, B. J. (2015, November 19). *What does it mean to be intersex?* NPR. https://www.npr.org/sections/13.7/2015/11/19/456458790/what-does-it-mean-to-be-intersex

King, M. L., Jr. (2012). *In a single garment of destiny: A global vision of justice.* Beacon Press.

Lane, H. (1979). *The wild boy of Aveyron.* Harvard University Press.

Lareau, A., & Weininger, E. B. (2009). *Paradoxical pathways: An ethnographic extension of Kohn's findings on class and childrearing.* Journal of Marriage and Family, 71(3).

Laughlin, L., Anderson, Martinez, A., & Gayfield, A., & (2021). *22 million employed in health care fight against COVID-19.* U.S. Census Bureau. https://www.census.gov/library/stories/2021/04/who-are-our-health-care-workers.html

Lengermann, M. P., & Niebrugge. G (2007). *The women founders: Sociology and social theory 1830–1930.* Waveland Press.

Lenin, V. (1916). *Imperialism, the highest stage of capitalism: A popular outline.* https://www.marxists.org/archive/lenin/works/1916/imp-hsc/imperialism.pdf

Lewontin, R. C. (1972). *The apportionment of human diversity.* Committee on Evolutionary Biology, University of Chicago.

Lim, D. (2020). *I'm embracing the term 'people of the global majority.'* Medium. https://regenerative.medium.com/im-embracing-the-term-people-of-the-global-majority-abd1c1251241

Lindsey, L. L. (2016). *Gender roles: A sociological perspective* (6th ed.). Routledge.

Linnaeus, C. (1735). *A General System of Nature, Through the Three Grand.* (12th ed.). Salvius.

Lopez, G. (2021, April 2). *Police officers are prosecuted for murder in less than 2 percent of fatal shootings.* Vox. https://www.vox.com/21497089/derek-chauvin-george-floyd-trial-police-prosecutions-black-lives-matter

Louati, Y. (2023). *CFA Franc: The "colonial currency" keeping 14 African nations on a leash.* https://www.trtworld.com/opinion/cfa-franc-the-colonial-currency-keeping-14-african-nations-on-a-leash-63270

Macionis, J. J. (2015). *Sociology: The basics.* Pearson.

Marx, K. & Engels, F. (1848). *The Communist manifesto.* The Communist League.

Marx, K. (1906). Capital: A Critique of Political Economy. New York Modern Library.

Meneses, P. Y. (2023). *Díaz-Canel: Cuban people are the protagonists of the victory in the national elections.* Granma. https://en.granma.cu/cuba/2023-04-06/diaz-canel-cuban-people-are-the-protagonists-of-the-victory-in-the-national-elections

Mills, C. W. (1956). *The power elite.* Oxford University Press.

Mills, C. W. (1959). *The Sociological Imagination.* Oxford University Press.

Milman, O. (2023, May 19). *New York City is sinking due to weight of its skyscrapers, new research finds.* The Guardian. https://www.theguardian.com/us-news/2023/may/19/new-york-city-sinking-skyscrapers-climate-crisis

Mindich, T. (2014, July 10). *More than half the world's population lives in urban areas, UN report finds.* PBS Newshour. https://www.pbs.org/newshour/world/half-worlds-population-live-urban-areas-un-report-finds

Morris, A. (2017). *The scholar denied: W.E.B Dubois and the birth of modern sociology.* University of California Press.

Müller-Wille, S. (2014). *Race and history: Comments from an epistemological point of view.* Science, Technology, and Human Values, Vol 39 (No. 4), pages 597-606. https://www.jstor.org/stable/i40147475

National Conference of State Legislators. (2023). *Voter ID laws*. https://www.ncsl.org/elections-and-campaigns/voter-id

National Institutes of Health. (2007, April 2). *NIDA survey shows lack of substance abuse treatment options for offenders*. https://www.nih.gov/news-events/news-releases/nida-survey-shows-lack-substance-abuse-treatment-options-offenders

National Sexual Violence Resource. (n.d.). *Statistics*. https://www.nsvrc.org/statistics

Naumann, E. (2020). *South Africa's new status as a "developed country" for purposes of United States' subsidies and countervailing duty investigations*. Tralac. https://www.tralac.org/blog/article/14567-south-africa-s-new-status-as-a-developed-country-for-purposes-of-united-states-subsidies-and-countervailing-duty-investigations

Neeley, L. (2023). *Cuba's new family code, a law of love*. Workers World. https://www.workers.org/2023/01/68708/

Newman, D. M. (2017). *Sociology: Exploring the architecture of everyday life*. SAGE.

Newman, M. D. (2012). *Sociology: Exploring the architecture of everyday life* (9th ed.). SAGE.

Nielson Company. (2018). *The Nielsen total audience report: Q1 2018*. https://www.nielsen.com/us/en/insights/report/2018/q1-2018-total-audience-report/

Nilsen, E. (2023, March 7). *What to know about the controversial Willow oil drilling project in Alaska*. CNN. https://www.cnn.com/2023/03/07/politics/willow-project-alaska-oil-explained-climate/index.html

Nishizawa, L. (2022, August 24). *How does U.S. voter turnout compare to the rest of the world's?* https://www.cfr.org/in-brief/how-does-us-voter-turnout-compare-rest-worlds

Norton Cyber Security. (2018). What is cyberbullying and what are the warning signs. Norton. https://us.norton.com/blog/kids-safety/what-is-cyberbullying

Norton, B. (2023). *BRICS challenges US "dollar dominance," Saudi considers selling oil in other currencies: New multipolar economic order*. Geopolitical Economy Report. https://geopoliticaleconomy.com/2023/01/21/brics-us-dollar-saudi-oil-currency-multipolar/

Norwood, C. (2021, April 23). *How infrastructure has historically promoted inequality*. PBS Newshour. https://www.pbs.org/newshour/politics/how-infrastructure-has-historically-promoted-inequality

Office of the United Nations High Commissioner for Human Rights. (2009). *The right to adequate housing*. United Nations. https://documents.un.org/doc/undoc/gen/g09/109/71/pdf/g0910971.pdf?token=YsXvUnZdrSjCpyhLsp&f=true

Olow, F. (2019). *The history of how Muslim women helped to overturn football's hijab ban*. gal-dem. https://gal-dem.com/this-is-the-history-of-how-muslim-women-helped-to-overturn-the-fifa-football-hijab-ban/

Owens, A. (2018). *Income segregation between school districts and inequality in students' achievement*. Sociology of Education, 91(1), 1–27. https://www.asanet.org/wp-content/uploads/attach/journals/jan18soefeature.pdf

Oyěwùmí, O. (1997). *The invention of women: Making an African sense of Western gender discourses*. University of Minnesota Press.

Paice, E. (2020). *By 2050, a quarter of the world's people will be African—this will shape our future*. The Guardian. https://www.theguardian.com/global-development/2022/jan/20/by-2050-a-quarter-of-the-worlds-people-will-be-african-this-will-shape-our-future

Parenti, C. (2013). *A radical approach to the climate crisis*. Dissent Magazine. https://www.dissentmagazine.org/article/a-radical-approach-to-the-climate-crisis

Party for Socialism and Liberation. (2022). *Socialist reconstruction: A better future for the United States*. Party for Socialism and Liberation Publications.

People's Dispatch. (2022). *Cubans just ratified the world's most progressive family code*. https://peoplesdispatch.org/2022/09/26/cubans-just-ratified-the-worlds-most-progressive-family-code/

Pew Research Center. (2015, April 2). *The future of world religions: Population growth projections, 2010–2050*. https://www.pewresearch.org/religion/2015/04/02/religious-projections-2010-2050/

Pew Research Center. (2019). *America in 2050*. https://www.pewresearch.org/social-trends/2019/03/21/america-in-2050/

Pew Research Center. (2021). *Beyond Red vs. Blue: The Political Typology*. Pew Research Center. https://www.pewresearch.org/politics/2021/11/09/beyond-red-vs-blue-the-political-typology-2/

Pew Research Center. (2021, October 28). *In U.S., far more support than oppose separation of church and state*. https://www.pewresearch.org/religion/2021/10/28/in-u-s-far-more-support-than-oppose-separation-of-church-and-state/

Philbrick, I. P. (2022). *A pro-religion Court*. The New York Times. https://www.nytimes.com/2022/06/22/briefing/supreme-court-religion.html

Pines, M. (1981). *The civilizing of Genie*. https://kccesl.tripod.com/genie.html

Quinlan, J. (2004, December 7). *Behind the sinking dollar: America's image as a "rogue nation?" What will it take to stop the U.S. dollar's slide?* The Globalist. https://www.theglobalist.com/behind-the-sinking-dollar-americas-image-as-a-rogue-nation/

Reid, K. (2023, September 5). *2010 Haiti earthquake: Facts, FAQs, and how to help*. World Vision. https://www.worldvision.org/disaster-relief-news-stories/2010-haiti-earthquake-facts

Reynolds, E. (2021). *A sociology reader: Foundational concepts for the introductory student*. Cognella.

Ritzer, G. (2014). *The McDonaldization of society*. SAGE.

Robinson, K., & Merrow, W. (2020). *The Arab Spring at ten years: What's the legacy of the uprisings?* Council on Foreign Relations. https://www.cfr.org/article/arab-spring-ten-years-whats-legacy-uprisings

Rodney, W. (1972). *How Europe underdeveloped Africa*. Verso.

Rodney, W. (2019). *The groundings with my brothers*. Verso. Originally published 1969

Rothstein, R. (2018). *The color of law*. Liveright.

Ruehl, J. P. (2022, September 28). *Understanding Libya's relentless destabilization*. Asia Times. https://asiatimes.com/2022/09/understanding-libyas-relentless-destabilization/

Salituro, C. (2020). *Reading primary research: Sociology research lesson 4*. Ways of Thinking: A Blog for Teaching Sociology. https://sociologysal.blogspot.com/2020_08_30_archive.html?m=0

Servet, Y. (2023). *Which countries have the most strikes in Europe and what impact does it have on the economy?* Euronews.net. https://www.euronews.com/next/2023/03/07/industrial-action-in-france-and-the-uk-which-countries-have-the-most-strikes-in-europe

Slave Voyages Consortium. (2021). *Trans-Atlantic slave trade database*. Slave Voyages. https://www.slavevoyages.org/voyage/database

Smith. W. (1988). *Three Latin American sociologists: Gino Germani, Pablo Gonzalez Casanova, Fernando Henrique Cardoso.* Journal of Interamerican Studies and World Affairs, 30(1), Cambridge University Press.

So. Y. A. (2015). *Sociology in East Asia.* In Kathleen Odell Korgen, The Cambridge Handbook of Sociology, (pgs. 1-29). Cambridge University Press.

Solomon, M. (2020). *What would "housing as a human right" look like in California?* KQED. https://www.kqed.org/news/11801176/what-would-housing-as-a-human-right-look-like-in-california

Starr, A. (2015). *Pork. It's what's for dinner once more at federal prisons.* NPR. https://www.npr.org/sections/thetwo-way/2015/10/16/449180734/pork-its-whats-for-dinner-once-more-at-federal-prisons

Stromquist, N. P. (2007). *The gender socialization process in schools: A cross-national comparison.* Education for All Global Monitoring Report 2008.

Taggart, E. (2020). *Finland solves its homelessness by providing apartments for anyone who needs one.* My Modern Met. https://mymodernmet.com/housing-first-finland-homelessness/

The Economist. (2022). Grub's up: *Why eating more insects might be good for the planet and good for you.* https://www.economist.com/graphic-detail/2013/05/14/grubs-up

Thomas, D., & Thomas, W. I. (1928). *The child in America.* Oxford University Press.

Tolbert, J., Drake, P., & Amico, A. (2022). *Key facts about the uninsured population.* Kaiser Family Foundation. https://www.kff.org/uninsured/issue-brief/key-facts-about-the-uninsured-population/

Totenberg, N., & McCammon, S. (2022). *Supreme Court overturns Roe v. Wade, ending right to abortion upheld for decades.* NPR. https://www.npr.org/2022/06/24/1102305878/supreme-court-abortion-roe-v-wade-decision-overturn

Tuck, E. & Yang, W. K. (2012). *Decolonization is not a metaphor.* Decolonization: Indigeneity, Education & Society, 1(1), 1–40. https://clas.osu.edu/sites/clas.osu.edu/files/Tuck%20and%20Yang%202012%20Decolonization%20is%20not%20a%20metaphor.pdf

U.S. Bureau of Labor Statistics (2021). *Labor force statistics from the current population survey.* https://www.bls.gov/cps/cpsaat11.htm

U.S. Census Bureau. (2022, February 24). *Census Bureau releases new educational attainment data.* https://www.census.gov/newsroom/press-releases/2022/educational-attainment.html

U.S. Census Bureau. (2022a). *Census Bureau releases new estimates on America's families and living arrangements.* https://www.census.gov/newsroom/press-releases/2022/americas-families-and-living-arrangements.html

U.S. Census Bureau. (2022b). *Census Bureau releases new report on living arrangements of children.* https://www.census.gov/newsroom/press-releases/2022/living-arrangements-of-children.html

U.S. Department of Housing and Urban Development. (2020). *Continuum of care: Homeless assistance programs, homeless populations and subpopulations.* https://files.hudexchange.info/reports/published/CoC_PopSub_NatlTerrDC_2020.pdf

Uggen, C. Larson, R., Shannon, S., & Stewart, R. (2022, October 25). *Locked out 2022: Estimates of people denied voting rights.* The Sentencing Project. https://www.sentencingproject.org/reports/locked-out-2022-estimates-of-people-denied-voting-rights/

Unger, N. C. (2008). *Superdelegates: An obstacle on the road to democratic elections.* https://origins.osu.edu/history-news/superdelegates-obstacle-road-democratic-elections?language_content_entity=en

United Healthcare Community Plan (2021). *What is Medicaid and what does it cover?* https://www.uhccommunityplan.com/dual-eligible/benefits/medicaid

United Nations Human Rights Council. (2009). Welcome to the United Nations. https://documents.un.org/doc/undoc/gen/g09/109/71/pdf/g0910971.pdf?token=DckRJhzexbr6L2Gwz1&fe=true

University of Michigan Center for Sustainable Systems (2021). *U.S. environmental footprint factsheet.* https://css.umich.edu/publications/factsheets/sustainability-indicators/us-environmental-footprint-factsheet

Vargas-Rios, M., Ramirez, R., & Jones, N. (2022). *Improved race and ethnicity measures reveal U.S. population is much more multiracial.* U.S. Census Bureau. https://www.census.gov/library/stories/2021/08/improved-race-ethnicity-measures-reveal-united-states-population-much-more-multiracial.html

Vedder, R. & Strehle, J. (2017). *The Diminishing Returns of a College Degree.* The Wall Street Journal. https://www.wsj.com/articles/the-diminishing-returns-of-a-college-degree-1496605241

Vemulakonda, S. (2021). *Why do brands continue to exploit Black and Brown women?* re/make. https://remake.world/stories/news/why-do-brans-continue-to-exploit-black-and-brown-women/

Villanueva, P. (2019). *Why decolonial feminism: New possibilities from Abya Yala.* https://towardfreedom.org/story/archives/women/why-decolonial-feminism-new-possibilities-from-abya-yala/

Violence Policy Center. (2020). *When men murder women.* https://vpc.org/studies/wmmw2020.pdf

W3Techs Web Technology Surveys. (2021). *Usage of content languages broken down by web servers.* https://w3techs.com/technologies/cross/content_language/web_server

Wadley, J. (2022). *Privileges confirmed for straight white men working in STEM.* Vice President for Communications, Michigan University. https://news.umich.edu/privileges-confirmed-for-straight-white-men-working-in-stem/

Wadud, A. (1999). *Qur'an and woman.* Oxford University Press.

Wallerstein, I. (2008). Global Stratification. In John. J. Macionis (12th ed.). *Sociology (pgs. 303-327).* Pearson.

Wang, Y. (2018). *China will "never seek hegemony," Xi says in reform speech.* AP News. https://apnews.com/article/4c9476378e184f238845337ba442715c

Weber, M. (1912). Authority and Autonomy in Marriage. In Elizabeth Kirchen, Selections from Marianne Weber's Reflections on Women and Women's Issues (pp. 27-41). J.C. B. Mohr

Weber, M. (1978). *Economy and society: An outline of interpretive sociology* (G. Roth & C. Wittich, Eds.). University of California Press. Original work published 1921

Weber, M. (1992). *The Protestant ethic and the spirit of capitalism.* Routledge Classics.

Weber, M. (2019). Global Stratification. In James M. Henslin (14th ed.), *Sociology A Down-to-Earth Approach (pgs. 189-219).* Pearson.

Webster, E. (2004). *Sociology in South Africa: Its past, present and future.* Society in Transition, 35(1).

Wehle, K. (2022). *The Supreme Court wants to end the separation of church and state.* Politico. https://www.politico.com/news/magazine/2022/08/10/supreme-court-separation-of-church-and-state-00050571

Wells-Barnett, Ida. B. (1892). *Southern Horrors.* Bedford Books.

Wells-Barnett, Ida. B. (1895). *A Red Record.* Bedford Books.

Williams, V. (2017). *Maxine Waters inspires a new anthem: "Reclaiming my time."* The Washington Post. https://www.washingtonpost.com/news/post-nation/wp/2017/08/01/maxine-waters-inspires-a-new-anthem-reclaiming-my-time/

Women's Media Center. (2021, November 18). *The status of women in the U.S. media.* https://womensmediacenter.com/reports/the-status-of-women-in-the-u-s-media-2021-1

World Bank (2020). *Egypt: World Bank provides US $400 million in support of universal health insurance system.* https://www.worldbank.org/en/news/press-release/2020/06/16/egypt-world-bank-provides-us-400-million-in-support-of-universal-health-insurance-system

Xinhua. (2021). *How China has lifted nearly 300 mln people out of poverty.* Xinhuanet. http://www.xinhuanet.com/english/2021-04/06/c_139862741.htm

Yeagley, R. M. (2020, November 9). *Why Native American reservations are the most poverty-stricken lands in America.* Foundation for Economic Education. https://fee.org/articles/why-native-american-reservations-are-the-most-poverty-stricken-lands-in-america/

Zimmerman, D., & West, C. (1987). Doing gender. *Gender and Society, 1*(2), 121–151. https://www.gla.ac.uk/0t4/crcees/files/summerschool/readings/WestZimmerman_1987_DoingGender.pdf

Zittleman, R. K., & Sadker, D. (2009). *Still failing at fairness: How gender bias cheats girls and boys in school and what we can do about it.* Scribner.

Printed in the USA
CPSIA information can be obtained
at www.ICGtesting.com
LVHW062252300824
789663LV00019B/63